Poems From The West Country

Edited by Heather Killingray

First published in Great Britain in 2007 by:
Young Writers
Remus House
Coltsfoot Drive
Peterborough
PE2 9JX
Telephone: 01733 890066
Website: www.youngwriters.co.uk

All Rights Reserved

© Copyright Contributors 2007

SB ISBN 978-1 84431 262 7

Foreword

This year, the Young Writers' *Away With Words* competition proudly presents a showcase of the best poetic talent selected from thousands of up-and-coming writers nationwide.

Young Writers was established in 1991 to promote the reading and writing of poetry within schools and to the young of today. Our books nurture and inspire confidence in the ability of young writers and provide a snapshot of poems written in schools and at home by budding poets of the future.

The thought, effort, imagination and hard work put into each poem impressed us all and the task of selecting poems was a difficult but nevertheless enjoyable experience.

We hope you are as pleased as we are with the final selection and that you and your family continue to be entertained with *Away With Words Poems From The West Country* for many years to come.

Contents

Yasmin Powell (11)   1

Bishops' College, Gloucester
Paige Gough (12)	2
Brandon Westcarr (12)	4
Jade Presley (13)	5
Roni Vizor & Lucy (13)	5
Roxanne Gardner (13)	6
Anthony Hall (15)	7
Lydia King (12)	8
Jamie Neate (13)	8
Harriette Wrightson & Sophie Clack (12)	9
Stacey Smith (12)	9

Bredon School, Tewkesbury
Jake Martin (15)	10

Broadlands School, Bristol
Elina Inanloo (16)	11

Chester Park Junior School, Bristol
Kaiesha Stewart-Haugh (11)	12
Daniel English (11)	13
William Millard (10)	13
Laura Kozak (11)	14
Tom Elsbury (11)	14
Ajay Singh (11)	15
Emma Kendall (11)	15
Erin Panes (11)	16
Tyler Cains (11)	16
Anna Martin (11)	17
Connor Nelmes (11)	17
Laura Crimp (11)	18
Ellie Howell (11)	18
Hannah Winkworth (10)	19
Luke Templeman (11)	19

Katrina Russell (11)   20
Jamie Houghton (10)   20

Chipping Campden School, Chipping Campden
Sam McQuail (13)   21
William Stewart (14)   22
Jessica Stamp (13)   22
Oliver Simpson (13)   23
Laurel Jones (13)   23
Kelly Baker (14)   24
David Halperin (13)   25
Bryony Nickson (12)   26
Rosie Tombs (13)   27

Cirencester Kingshill School, Cirencester
Nick Mellor (13)   27
James O'Leary (13)   28
Joe Morris (12)   29
Harry Carter (12)   29
Charley Yates (13)   30
Rosie Mizon (13)   30
Rebecca Hicks (12)   31
Lucy Watkins (14)   31
Joanne Alderman (13)   32
Harry Rhys-Thomas (12)   32
James Piatek (12)   33
Kirsten McKechnie (12)   33
Jade Mathieson (12)   34
Alex Hibbs (13)   34
Oliver Newman (13)   35
Rachel Ody (13)   35
Katie Mackenzie (12)   36
Isaac Herbert (12)   37
Katrin Lager (13)   38
Luke Barton (13)   38
Jess Logan (12)   39
Jess Hollister (13)   39
Joshua Baker (12)   40
James Bellringer (13)   41
Charlotte Williams (12)   41
Ben Mixture (13)   42

Laura Cox (12)	43
Sapphire Rogers (12)	44
Kate Godwin (13)	44
Charlotte Morris (13)	45
Elliot Mace (11)	45
Lauren Gleed (13)	46
Ryan Curtis (12)	46
Jake House (13)	47
George Jones (12)	47
Alex Lane (13)	48
Chelsea Collins (12)	48
Jamie Gordon-Walker (13)	49
Hannah Devine (11)	49
Paul Allen (13)	50
John Limb (12)	50
Katie Hobbs (13)	51
Luke Oosthuizen (13)	51
Daniella Keen (12)	52
Thomas Woods (13)	52
Tom Sargent (13)	53
Stuart Evans (13)	54
Rosie O'Connor (11)	54
Jennifer Benton (13)	55
Marcus Rhodes (13)	55
Siobhan Walker (13)	56
John Cornwell (13)	56
Jonathan Sampson (12)	57
Bethany Tindale (11)	57
Andrew Hartnell (12)	58
Lynn Kirkpatrick (12)	58
Jeanie Whelan (12)	59
Joshua Wall (12)	59
Grace Kinsey (12)	60
James Barry (13)	61
Lewis Evans (12)	62
Toni Mottram (13)	62
Megan Saunders (13)	63
Emma Legg (12)	63
Abbie Ho (12)	64
Robert Fowkes (11)	64
Nicole Brookes (12)	65
Abby Beasley (12)	65

Tom Gardiner (13)	66
Elouise Ody (13)	66
Jodie Fletcher (12)	67
Dale Wall (13)	68
Laura Outram (13)	68
Amy Chinnock (13)	69
Oliver Lendon (13)	69
Carrie Bloodworth (13)	70
Bradley Robinson (13)	70
Katie Moore (12)	71
Tuesday Townsend (12)	71
Clare Wynn-Mackenzie (13)	72
Rose Burston (12)	72

Cotham School, Bristol

Caitlin McWilliams	73
Evie Miles	74
Tom Last (12)	75
Connel McLaughlin (13)	76
Kate Brennan (12)	77
Jake Thompson (12)	78
Thomas Jenkins (15)	79
Josie Brown	80

Culverhay School, Bath

Nick Henden (15)	80
James Eynon (14)	81
Peter Calley (14)	82
Joe Payne (14)	83

Lakers School, Coleford

Paul Yearley (13)	83

Rowdeford School, Devizes

Mirelle Cross-Jones & Georgina Turton (14)	84
William Filer (15)	84
Eden Saunders (15)	84
Craig Lundberg (15)	85

St Benedict's Catholic Sports College, Cheltenham
Hannah Landon-Hammond (12) 85
Cameron Smith (12) 86
Lauren Randell (12) 87
Tanya Tucker 88
Charlotte Davies (13) 88
Elizabeth Hart (12) 89
Scott Boon 89
Michaella Rayson 90
Sam Morgan (14) 91
Kyle Smith 92
Dylan Pezzack 92
Liam Powell (12) 93
Alistair Potter (12) 93
Claire Grey (12) 94
Callum Brooks 94
Joe Horsted (12) 95
Charlotte Randall (12) 95
Stephen Oldroyd (11) 96
Lauren Quemby (12) 97
Aaron Walker (12) 98
Ryan Pearce-Smith (11) 98
Emma Stephens 99
Rebekah Swain (13) 99
Megan Davis 100
Aaron Pearce (12) 100
Kim Rayner (12) 101
Tessa Dainty (12) 102
Abby Martin 103
Marinel Kristine Jocson 104
Michael Davis 105
Julia White (13) 106
Jordan Randall (13) 107
Lindsay Waters (13) 108
Dipika Patel 109

South Wilts Grammar School for Girls, Salisbury
Hannah Shearer (15) 110
Rachel Warne (17) 111
Imogen Copp (16) 112
Anna MacDiarmid (16) 113

Paige Christie (15)	114
Iona MacDonald (15)	115
Lydia Sargent (15)	116
Mei Ling Henry (14)	117
Clare Hillier (17)	118
Nadine Rowe (16)	119
Melissa Blair Denton (17)	120
Sîan Kerley (14)	121
Freya Webb (14)	122
Rachel Beagrie (15)	123
Evie Kitt (15)	123
Ruth-Megan Spreadbury (17)	124
Catherine Honor (15)	125
Natasha Cowley (15)	126

The Castle School, Thornbury

Sophie Romain (11)	126
Kiddie Sheikh (12) & Sam Steele (11)	127
Paige Sanders (12) & Cate Welmers (12)	128
Katie Walker (12)	129
Sam Crow (12) & Ryan Waite (11)	130
Hannah Moore (12)	131
Sam Mindenhall (11)	132
Richard Timbrell (11)	133
Paul James Long (12)	134
Hannah Cornford (12)	135

Westonbirt School, Tetbury

Helen Walpole (11)	135
Cassie Jane Greenhill (12)	136
Lucy Fenn (12)	136
Lydia Marshall (11)	137
Megan Mardon (13)	137
Emma Gardner (12)	138
Hester Ingram (11)	139

The Poems

The Three Of Us!

My favourite person,
I have two,
A lucky girl I am,
I always knew!
Keri, Charlotte and I
We're an inseparable team,
We'd chill out at the park for an hour,
Or hide and seek in bushes of green.
When we're at school,
We still have hours of fun,
We talk, talk, talk,
Or go round the field for a run.
We laugh together,
We cry together,
But most of all we love each other.
Keri and Charlotte,
They're like sisters to me,
Except they're more fun than my sisters will ever be!
If I had to describe them in five words,
Those five words below you will see,
Fantastic . . . amazing . . . weird . . . wacky . . . and the
Best friends anyone could ever dream of!
They also make me giggle with glee.
My special message to them will be,
That I would circle the world to find you,
You will always stay in my heart
And you will also always stay my friend,
Even if we have difficulty or we come to a dead end!

Yasmin Powell (11)

Me, Myself And I

I came into this world
Crash, bang, boom!
Kicking and screaming
From out of the womb.

I was only small
Six pounds in weight
I was on time
I wasn't born late.

Mum told me
There was so much pain
And she said over and over
'Never again!'

When I was born
There wasn't much money
But Mum always made sure
There was food in my tummy.

I learnt how to eat
I learnt how to talk
I learnt how to crawl
And I learnt how to walk.

I learnt how to play
With girls and boys
I didn't mind them
Sharing my toys.

I grew from toddler to child
And over the years
There was lots of laughter
And very few tears.

I started school at the age of four
Mum left me at the classroom door
I was worried at first I have to say
But I loved it from that very first day.

Mum wanted more children
Now we are three
I have two brothers
No sisters for me.

Both were born
On the very same date
And both were born
At the very same weight.

I have two dippy dogs
All shaggy and big
They should have been hogs
Because they eat like pigs.

I like sports
Being part of a team
But I don't like homework
If you know what I mean.

Football is my favourite game
How about you?
Who do you support?
I support Man U.

When I leave school
Not quite yet
I'll pass all my exams
To become a vet.

I want to travel the world
And have a great time
Live my life as I like
And I'll be just fine.

Paige Gough (12)
Bishops' College, Gloucester

A Darkness Engulfs Us

The world is changing
We can't stop it or control it
We try and harness it, but fail
And in doing so we corrupt it
Only making it worse.

The sun glares down scorching the land
Waves break against the land
Making it crumble away
We're at the brink of existence
Feebly crumbling away
On a dying planet.

The scientists try and tell us
But the ones with power ignore them
And keep taking from Mother Earth
Their greed will be their undoing.

People are dying alongside their animal brethren
The proud prince - lion
The wacky wonder - monkey
The poor pauper - man
Dying together.

Soon all will be gone
Nothing left *as darkness engulfs us*
And when that time comes
Oblivion will be our only destiny.

Stop poverty! Stop animal cruelty!
Stop slavery! Stop war and fighting!
And stop global warming!
Before it stops you . . .

Brandon Westcarr (12)
Bishops' College, Gloucester

Teenage Life

Teenage life is really hard!
You get picked on and called *fat lards!*

Teenage life can be fun
When you're old you can laugh
And think what you have done!

Teenage life can be boring
Like when you're in science
You have to do silly drawings!

Teenage life can be cool
Like in the summer when
You're chilling in the pool!

Teenage life can be sad
When you look back and
Think what a great bunch of friends you had.

Jade Presley (13)
Bishops' College, Gloucester

Teenagers Today

Teenagers love to shop
And they love the music hip hop.

Teenagers like to meet their mates
Outside their school gates.

Some teenagers take drugs
And some are mean thugs.

Teenagers love their lives
Some are husbands, some wives.

Even though this is stupid
They must be struck by Cupid.

Girls are loving the brand new fashion
Boys love football, that's their passion.

Roni Vizor & Lucy (13)
Bishops' College, Gloucester

Being Young

Being young is totally fun.
In the summer we like to play in the sun.
Being young we can have lots of sweets
And don't get much sleep,
Because we like to stay up late.
We can be very healthy, but not very wealthy.
Privacy is what I like
And I like to ride my bike.
My bike gives me freedom.
I like being energetic
And my brother's so pathetic.
In school we can be immature
But we still do our chore.
We all fight with brothers and sisters
Because they can be such a pain.
At least us kids don't have to wear false teeth,
Like our grandmothers did.
Dressing in cool clothes
Is different to what the world knows.
Having a boyfriend and girlfriend is OK,
But when you break apart,
It really breaks our heart.
At Easter we get lots of chocolate
And a lot of homework.

Roxanne Gardner (13)
Bishops' College, Gloucester

Year 10

Goes quite fast
Listening to teacher's words
Saying stuff like 'do coursework'
Getting on our nerves

None of us disciplined
Clock going round and round
Sitting down ignoring ole' teach'
All I hear is sounds

Going on for evermore
Bored out of our brains
Pen running out
And driving us insane

Working really hard
Struggling to be prepared
Test will be here soon
Getting scared

Tests have arrived
They aren't going to get done
All I can say now is
I hope Year 11 is more fun.

Anthony Hall (15)
Bishops' College, Gloucester

Teenage Life!

Teenage life is really hard
You get called these names
'Sluts, hoes and tarts'.

You have those girls that think they're hard
You stand up for yourself
They run faster than cars.

You have to do your
SATs, exams, GCSEs
You have to watch these silly films
About bumblebees.

Teenage life is really cool
You get your gossip
And girl phone calls.

You get to have slumber parties
And get your nails and hair done
You can sit and watch chick flicks
And have lots of fun!

Lydia King (12)
Bishops' College, Gloucester

School Life

Pencils are bright
And they make you write.
Tall and thin
Then they go in the bin.
Pencil cases are so right
They make you equipped for school life.
Rubbers are big, bendy and floppy
Then you rub out mistakes and then it gets messy.
This is what you need for school life.

Jamie Neate (13)
Bishops' College, Gloucester

Sad And Alone

When I was little my baby brother died,
Then my parents decided to push me aside.
Then they argued, they split
And I went along with it,
And now I am left on the streets.

Heaps of time I spent alone,
Wandering the streets with no home.
I wanted my parents so much,
I wanted to feel their touch.
I needed their arms around me,
But I don't think they could see,
That without them, I am nothing
And; I will never be.

Harriette Wrightson & Sophie Clack (12)
Bishops' College, Gloucester

School

We're here for fun,
Not to get done.
We all got our pencil cases,
All flashy, bright and bold.

Lucky we're not doing PE in the cold,
Our teachers are fuzzy
And always in a tizzy,
Time is going slow.

There goes the whistle,
It's just been blown,
It's time to go home.

Stacey Smith (12)
Bishops' College, Gloucester

I Met A Girl . . .

I met a girl with golden hair
And skin soft to the touch,
I complimented her on this
She was flattered very much.
Her long, dark lashes flickered
And silky cheeks turned red,
A crisp, white smile revealed itself
As she timidly turned her head.

I began to make conversation
Then we talked about this and that,
From Stamford Bridge and music
To our brave lads in Iraq.
We walked some more into the night
Under moonlit trees,
My arm wrapped round her like a coat
To shelter her from the breeze.

After hours of tender discussion
In the heart of Gloucester town,
We became quite fond of each other
And in her, something I found.
Behind her hazel eyes
And beyond her burgundy lips,
Was a mind of great inspiration
And a heart that I'll never rip.

Jake Martin (15)
Bredon School, Tewkesbury

What Is Love?

Love is something, of which it's hard to say,
It cannot be drawn, described in any way
And one could say it does not mean a word,
But its meaning is felt, not smelt, tasted or heard.
What is love?

Love is a dream, a bubble from the heart,
An endless stream of which there is no start,
A silver star burning brighter than the sun,
It's given like a gift to everyone.
What is love?

Love is the cord that binds young couples' hands,
It can't be given by force or by command
For it's natural affection, warm and tender too,
Sweet as rose blossoms, fresh as morning dew.
What is love?

Love is 'Mum's' lullaby, a gentle mother's kiss,
And is the blanket that gives the baby bliss.
It's the tiny smiles innocent children give
And without love it would be hard to live.
What is love?

Love is so hot, it melts all hatred or woe
And is a thing we all deserve to know
For it is a warmth even animals can use,
Yet love would be a terrible thing to lose.
What is love?

But when not understood and not returned,
Love is the fire, blackening as it burns!
And when it is betrayed, or given with lies,
It can but bring hot tears to the eyes!
What is love?

Oh, such a word I have not seen before,
For finding love is like entering an enchanted door.
And yet it cannot be bough with money or gold,
It's freely given like a parcel left to unfold.
What is love?

It is the only way to live at rest,
And can be gained if we all try our best,
And though some feel they have no love to share,
If they look in their hearts, the love will be glowing there.
What is love?
Oh, what is love . . .

Elina Inanloo (16)
Broadlands School, Bristol

Without Me

Firstly I was excited,
About going to an English school.
My Trinidadian accent,
I thought they would think was cool.

But then just because of my colour,
I got called nasty names,
To me it wasn't at all friendly,
To them their coolest games.

I wanted to tell a teacher,
But they didn't seem to care,
Making fun of my accent,
I knew they didn't want me there.

So left on my own in a corner,
Is all I had left to do,
Most of the names I didn't understand,
I didn't have a clue.

Nothing could be done about it,
As far as they could see,
Their school would be a preferable place,
Without me.

Kaiesha Stewart-Haugh (11)
Chester Park Junior School, Bristol

Coming To England

All alone in the playground,
No one to play with,
Just me on my own.
Sadly walking around the playground,
Again and again.
When people walk past me,
They laugh and they stare,
Like I'm the odd one out.
All I want is a friend,
Who won't laugh or tease me.
A friend who won't treat me different
Because of my colour.
One day when I thought I had a friend,
They tricked me and then kicked me.
All alone in the playground,
No one to play with,
Just me on my own.

Daniel English (11)
Chester Park Junior School, Bristol

Inside Me

I'm hurt deep inside my heart,
Words flowing through my mind,
I hate human beings because they hurt my feelings,
Shouting in my ear bad things about my colour.

William Millard (10)
Chester Park Junior School, Bristol

Unexpected

Coming to England,
I thought it'd be great!
All the education
And finding some mates.

But they treated me like trash,
Because I didn't fit in,
Everyone left me by myself
And it felt like they threw me in the bin.

In class,
It was just the same.
They made fun of my race,
They treated it like a game.

They said words to me,
Which I didn't understand.
However, I knew they were spiteful,
Because they made unusual signs with their hands.

All in all,
Life in school was upsetting and unfair.
I didn't feel how I thought I'd feel,
I thought there'd be lots of love and care.

Laura Kozak (11)
Chester Park Junior School, Bristol

Coming To England

What do you mean?
I'm not dirty, I'm clean
You shouldn't make fun of me
You make me sound like an unwanted flea
You hate me, well I hate you
If I'm dirty, you are too!
Don't make fun of me
You make it sound like
I should be left to die at sea.

Tom Elsbury (11)
Chester Park Junior School, Bristol

Coming To England

Coming to England is very special to me
I get to meet my family
For my sister and me.

First I lived with my auntie
Now I've left Trinidad
To go see my marmie.

It was my first day at school
People made fun of me
Just because I wasn't cool.

I left Trinidad just for this
But it was worth it because
I had done it for my little sis.

Ajay Singh (11)
Chester Park Junior School, Bristol

Bad Days

No one likes me in school
Because I am uncool
I get beaten up every day
When I go out and play
The teacher hates me
In fact no one likes me
In school I'm scared, upset and lonely
There's no one for me to lean on
I have no friends
I'm full of dead ends
I have no one to talk to
No one says, 'How are you?'
I have loads of bad days
Because I am different!

Emma Kendall (11)
Chester Park Junior School, Bristol

Races From Different Places

My teacher thinks that just because I'm black
I am not meant to be where I am at

I miss Trinidad
Where I was born with my mum and dad

I love school
I love to learn

But when people bully me
It hurts so bad inside you see

Our neighbours move away from us
Not before flooding us

They called the police
I wish I could see my niece

In what year, in what day
Will people say
I'm sorry for today and yesterday?

Erin Panes (11)
Chester Park Junior School, Bristol

Coming To Britain

The boat journey was terrible,
I was in the bottom class,
Then a weird looking man took out his shiny, silver cutlass.
As I arrived in Britain, I was very, very queasy,
Because as I got off the boat, everything looked eerie!
I stumbled down the stairs in a lot of dismay,
All because of this boy who thought my colour was brown clay.
My suitcase happily gleaming, my face very appealing.
The customs were disrespectful, but I was very thoughtful.
I was thinking about my dad, whom I left in Trinidad.

Tyler Cains (11)
Chester Park Junior School, Bristol

Life In England

I go to bed each night
With tears left in my eyes,
Wishing I was in Trinidad
Where my happy spirit lies.

I go to school each morning
And try to make new friends,
Some spit spiteful words at me
The hope for happiness then ends.

I go home from school that evening
Hanging my head down low,
Marmie holds me close and kisses me
Then says she loves me so.

I try school again that morning
With a positive attitude,
The other kids don't like it
So are horrible and rude.

This has made me realise
People hate the colour of my race,
Neither do they care
If tears drip down my face.

Anna Martin (11)
Chester Park Junior School, Bristol

Why?

Why do people hound me with these malicious words?
Why is it that the colour of a man's skin
Holds one race inferior and the other superior?
Why is there such hatred for white or black?
Only when this barrier is destroyed,
Then and only then can we be united as one,
As a civilised nation.

Connor Nelmes (11)
Chester Park Junior School, Bristol

Who Am I?

Leaving Trinidad was heartbreaking,
No friends was I making.

Teacher called me a name,
Because I wasn't the same.

Children laughed at me,
That's when I began to see.

Brown!
That was my colour.

White!
That was their colour.

They did not like it,
That is how I had to sit.

Then that was the day,
In hot, sweltering May.

I did a lively dance,
It was a jiggling prance.

I had finally found people's *respect!*

Laura Crimp (11)
Chester Park Junior School, Bristol

Races In People's Faces

I get shouted at in my face
Because I am a different race.
They hurt my feelings really bad
I cry and cry, I'm very sad.
They don't know how it really feels
Sometimes they even steal.
They think I'm invisible
Like I'm not liveable.
I want to make friends
But if I do, it badly ends.
Colour doesn't matter!

Ellie Howell (11)
Chester Park Junior School, Bristol

I Don't Know!

I go to school each day,
Teachers thinking I'm nasty,
Calling me a guttersnipe,
Telling me to speak the Queen's language.

Up against the wall,
Racist things being spat at me,
Could not understand them,
But knew they were not nice.

Walking home,
On a cold evening,
Children laughing,
I'm crying.

I really hate this school
And really hate this country.

Hannah Winkworth (10)
Chester Park Junior School, Bristol

Coming To England

In the playground yesterday,
A boy shouted in my face,
I thought he wanted to play,
But it was something else.

I can't believe the things you said,
You of all people, Norman.
His face suddenly went bright red,
Then he walked away in shame.

I'm not dirty, I'm clean,
It's just the colour of my skin.
Do people stab me in the back
Just because I'm black?

Luke Templeman (11)
Chester Park Junior School, Bristol

I Hate!

I love school, I really do!
But no one ever cares,
All the children look at me,
But I hate the way they stare!

I know it's because of my colour
And the accent of my race,
I hate the way they call me names,
Just because of the colour of my face!

I get called a guttersnipe,
By my English teacher, Miss Sniss,
I go home and tell my marmie,
She smiles and gives me a kiss!

She says she loves me
And things in the world will change,
I wish I was in Trinidad,
With all my family and friends!

Katrina Russell (11)
Chester Park Junior School, Bristol

Her Colour

Just because she's black,
People stab her in the back.
There's a feeling right inside,
That you really can't unwind
And . . . it . . . hurts!

She has to take the excruciating pain,
So they don't get the better of her.
She sits down in the playground
Trying to make friends,
It would be nicer for her,
Even if they pretend.

Jamie Houghton (10)
Chester Park Junior School, Bristol

The Meaning Of Life

What does it all mean,
This bizarre, confusing life?
What is behind it?

What makes all of us,
Travel through this long journey?
What is behind it?

Are we blind to it?
Could it possibly be false?
What is behind it?

Or perhaps it's not,
Hidden away in some nook.
What is behind it?

Maybe it's in front,
Maybe it's no mystery.
What is behind it?

I think I know it,
The meaning is all so clear.
What is behind it?

The meaning to me,
Is just to live and enjoy.
That is behind it!

Sam McQuail (13)
Chipping Campden School, Chipping Campden

The Wrath Of The Shunned

It is a sad thing
To see a man who is exiled
Cast out by society
But a sadder thing still
To see a man succumb
To the rage and the wrath
Give up all trace of humanity
And become one of the shunned
Silently raging
Ready to burn
Ready to strike
Ready to die
For a man who has nothing to lose
Is the most dangerous of fiends
There are no devils or witches
Just the monsters of Man's making
The shunned and the damned.

William Stewart (14)
Chipping Campden School, Chipping Campden

This Is Love

The thought just flitters through the skies,
Your voice just echoes in my mind,
To see you with her breaks me apart,
The look in your eye shatters my heart.
Can't you see the hidden war I am fighting
Or the way I crumble when I see you smiling?
Sometimes I think of Noah and the dove,
But I know what this is . . .
This is love.

Jessica Stamp (13)
Chipping Campden School, Chipping Campden

How Rock Is Formed

I am metamorphic rock,
I come in layers,
Like the pattern on your sock.

I started life as a little pebble,
But the heat and pressure
Was incredible.

I am metamorphic rock,
I come in layers,
Like the pattern on your sock.

Look at my little crystals shine,
All of them are mine.

I am metamorphic rock,
I come in layers,
Like the pattern on your sock.

I go round and round,
But I hardly make a sound!

Oliver Simpson (13)
Chipping Campden School, Chipping Campden

A Rhyming Poem

Although alliteration
Is nothing but a noun,
It causes a sensation
When sizzling sausages make a sound!

With onomatopoeia
It isn't 'Just like that',
It yowls and howls and miaows and growls
and copies like a cat!

And the point of this short poem
is about the use of rhyme,
I'm sorry, I must go
as I have just run out of time!

Laurel Jones (13)
Chipping Campden School, Chipping Campden

Evolving Emotions

The darkness into which I gave you my heart,
Was the same darkness that made us separate,
My love for you still grows,
Like that of a newly sprung rose.

My eyes bathe themselves in sour tears,
Wishing that through this fog, my feelings are seen clear,
Inside each tear is some hope that you still love me,
But through time I seem unable to see,
That you move on without living in deceit,
My tears soon show that I feel beat.

Even though I feel dead,
I shall not lower my head,
As the tears I lost over you,
Were many weeks overdue,
You thought I didn't know about the lie,
But you are wrong, I merely cried at the fact I wanted you to die,
No one deserves to feel such sorrow,
So may I have that knife to borrow?
Which I shall plunge into your heart,
Now you know the pain you gave me in such a great art.

Your eyes release sour tears,
I now hope you can see clear,
The pain you caused me turned into hate,
You beg for my forgiveness but it's too late,
I turn around and walk through the door,
Never to see you anymore,
Your worthless corpse which remains on the bloodstained floor.

Kelly Baker (14)
Chipping Campden School, Chipping Campden

Ode To An Oldie

I was once very young,
With a functioning tongue,
I could even dig.

I kept some chickens,
Kept a rabbit
And I sold a pig.

My life was fine,
I drank good wine,
But now I am ninety-nine.

I live in a home,
Where the food tastes like foam
And the water has probably been peed in.

And now I am sad,
I haven't been bad,
But my family doesn't come to see me.

They live their lives,
As I used to,
When I was once as happy as you.

But they don't know,
That they will soon go
To the old folks home I live in.

And now I'm in my grave,
My name was Dave
And now I can go to Heaven!

David Halperin (13)
Chipping Campden School, Chipping Campden

Freak

They steal my books
They steal my money
They leave deep bruises on my white skin, like black paint on snow
They throw rotten food at my bedroom window
They force me to visit the hospital a lot
'Hey! Freak, come back! Don't run away you chicken!
We are going to get you for this!'

I don't mind, I'm used to it, it's my life, I can cope
But my mother cries through the night
Mum and Dad argue with each other when they think I'm not listening
Fighting grows . . . voices raised . . . hands raised . . .
Mum slaps Dad, even in front of me now.

One harsh winter, I come home from school
But I don't find Mum there
Dad says she is on holiday
I ask why
Dad says she needs a break. I know why.

Mum's room is a mess
What in the world has happened in here?
Pillows ripped, cupboards turned over
Dad's favourite vase smashed to ruins
A photo smashed on the floor, it's a picture of Mum, Dad and I
I was still a baby back then, Mum holding me in her arms
Dad's hand on her shoulder.

Dark scribbles over my face.

My heart stops beating the moment I see it
I know this was Mum's doing
Why did I not realise earlier?
Mum's cries in the night, Mum's arguments

It was entirely my fault
I'm sorry
I didn't mean to hurt you Mum
I didn't mean to be such a . . .

Freak.

Bryony Nickson (12)
Chipping Campden School, Chipping Campden

The Willowy Tree

There stands the tree, tall and proud.
There winds the river with its willowy shroud.
There run the rabbits, full of glee
And there stays my heart beside the willowy tree.

There is the ivy with its choking tight hold.
There is the oak tree, so incredibly old.
There dash the deer, from the hunt they must flee
And there stays my heart beside the willowy tree.

There goes the feeling of freedom and light
And the life that lives in the dead of night.
Still there creeps the predator, eager for tea,
But there stays my heart beside the willowy tree.

Rosie Tombs (13)
Chipping Campden School, Chipping Campden

War

What is war?
Arrows raining on the enemies,
Swords slashing the flesh off enemy's bones,
A gloomy graveyard of hell,
An everlasting wasteland of doom,
Broken bones, deadly wounds,
One big nightmare.
Cruelly killing men and boys,
Parents getting left behind,
War is a casualty maker,
Steel boxes under houses,
Big booms everywhere around you,
Loved ones falling dead,
Planes falling from the sky,
Heroes dying at random.

Nick Mellor (13)
Cirencester Kingshill School, Cirencester

The March

One . . . two . . . three,
I waver and fall,
My searing limbs wail, screeching icily with the
                              retching bombardments,
Fear swells, thriving within my bloated, shell-shocked veins,
My heart emerged to the steady beat of the march no more.

Four . . . five . . . six,
Rhythmical wails are crudely uttered from the urchins of the air,
                                        Messerschmitt dive,
Piercing, pelting the air with their searing bullets,
Drilling savagely into the tired earth, like the rain,
Which cackled eerily around it.

Seven . . .
I tremble again, fulfilled one what?
Tears well like a child's mind infiltrated by demons merged in
                                      malicious delirium.
My futile endeavour, a barrage of hatred, a volley of despise, why?
Why care . . . why love?
Our belief, our manifest has reformed.
Our passion and our dwindling desire has become a delinquent of
                                          our lives,
Court-martialled.

Eight . . . nine . . .
The pastures we fight for, the land we seek,
All gorged by the gluttonous entity, drooping and dripping across
                                      the rotting corpses,
Which were once the hordes of our hope.

Ten . . .
Power.

James O'Leary (13)
Cirencester Kingshill School, Cirencester

The Beautiful Day

It's a beautiful day,
The grass is green and the sky is blue,
The clouds are thick but the sun burns through,
The heather fills the rolling hills and the moss covers the rock,
As down below in endless fields, the shepherd rounds his flock.

The sky turns from blue to orange as the sun hangs low in the sky,
You sit beside a gentle stream and watch some birds go by,
You watch the fish in the shallow stream, the newts, the dragonfly,
As you stand to begin your journey home, you hear a familiar cry.
The cry of birds high in the trees, beside the gentle stream
And you wait and listen for a while to the sound of a peaceful dream.

The orange sun goes down and then the day is done,
But when the sun rises, the new day is begun.

Joe Morris (12)
Cirencester Kingshill School, Cirencester

The Steam Engine

The steam engine pulls away from the roadside,
Bellowing white smoke as it goes,
Choking all the passers-by as smoke goes up their nose,
Oil and grease spits over the driver, dirtying his clothes.

The steam engine chugs down the highway,
The fly wheel spinning madly,
As the coal glows in the boiler,
Heating up the water.

The water is now steam,
Whistling out of the piston,
Pushing it round to power the steam engine.
The steam engine is nearly out of steam,
It groans to a halt in a lay-by to fill up with water.

Harry Carter (12)
Cirencester Kingshill School, Cirencester

My Secret Garden

I walked along the stony path
Towards the place I like to go
Across the bridge
Down the stairs
Into the woods where the birds chirp

In the bushes was an old door
With a key shaped like an F
Through the door was a place
Where dreams are made and the sun sets.

Overnight the flowers grew
Roses
Tulips
And sunflowers too
In the middle is a swing
All of this and more is
My secret garden.

Charley Yates (13)
Cirencester Kingshill School, Cirencester

If I Were . . .

If I were a dog, I would live in a house
If I were a mouse, I would live in a hole
If I were a mole, I would live in a log
If I were a frog, I would live under a mat
If I were a cat, I would live at the sea
I think I will choose to be me!

Rosie Mizon (13)
Cirencester Kingshill School, Cirencester

My Horse

I walk over to the field,
Head collar and lead rope in hand,
I call my beautiful palomino,
As he gallops towards me,
His tail swishes in the breeze.

I gently put his bridle on,
Followed by the saddle,
Safely mounted, we trot into the school,
We fly over the jumps,
With his tail in the air.

As we finish, I take off his saddle,
Then the bridle,
I put his head collar on,
As we walked along the road,
His hooves went *clip, clop.*

Rebecca Hicks (12)
Cirencester Kingshill School, Cirencester

Sunset

Just after six,
The sunset begins,
With mixed colours in,
Makes it all bright and golden,
Everyone sat around,
Watching it go down slowly,
Red, orange, yellow,
A hint of blue and purple,
Makes everyone relax,
Calming, soothing, warm,
Makes it outstanding,
It makes it romantic
And fills the sky with red,
Silent, magical, colourful,
Makes it all peaceful.

Lucy Watkins (14)
Cirencester Kingshill School, Cirencester

The Witch

Night has come.
The scent of flowers rises up into the air.
The only bright star in the sky glows against the
                        pitch-black darkness.
The wind ruffles in my hair,
As our two bodies move as one.
She is my eyes as we run through the night,
Not knowing where we are going, just running.
Her flanks rubbed against me,
Our sweat mixed together,
It was as if we had become one.

We're running from her,
The witch,
The demon,
The slayer.
Evil sucks you in if you stay with her.
She had everyone fooled,
Apart from us.
We're free
And always will be.
Night is our cover.

Joanne Alderman (13)
Cirencester Kingshill School, Cirencester

Nursery

Running around like nothing mattered
Until you were asked out, then you were flattered
The relationship lasted only a day
Then you were back to your normal play
Your last day at the school
You all had a swim in a huge, huge pool
Then it was time to get dry
So you all said a happy bye-bye.

Harry Rhys-Thomas (12)
Cirencester Kingshill School, Cirencester

Football

Children playing football
They kick and pass the ball
They're heading for each other's goals
To score the winning goal.

If you commit to a tackle
You must make sure you're right
Because if you miss the ball
The player will be out of sight.

You have to play as a team
Unless you want to lose
Because if that is what happens
The team will have the blues.

Our striker, Bob
Made his own luck
He scored the winning penalty
And won us the cup.

James Piatek (12)
Cirencester Kingshill School, Cirencester

Drip, Drap

Dewing fields,
Seeding fields,
Ginormous, evergreen trees,
Birds cheeping in the branches of an old oak tree,
A pine cone falling gently but slowly to the ground,
Clouds coming in,
Drip, drap,
Tip, tap,
Here come the raindrops,
No sun is near, heard or seen, no sight, dark clouds.

Kirsten McKechnie (12)
Cirencester Kingshill School, Cirencester

Raining Friendship

When I look outside this big, round window,
I can see the rain and everybody outside,
Running, walking, skipping.

If I was outside with you,
I would offer you my umbrella,
However, if you choose to get wet,
Then I shall get wet too.

If it was raining,
I would rather get my wellies
And skip in the puddles with you,
Then hide under an umbrella to stop getting wet.

This thing here is called friendship,
Nothing more, nothing less.

So when I look outside this big, round window,
I see the rain and my friendship.

Jade Mathieson (12)
Cirencester Kingshill School, Cirencester

The Beach

I feel the soft sand,
Running through my toes,
With the palm trees swaying above my head,
Fishes swimming on the seabed,
As the sun beams down,
The lifeguards are out,
To save children,
So they don't drown.

Alex Hibbs (13)
Cirencester Kingshill School, Cirencester

Twickenham
(Home of England rugby)

The roar of the crowd
As I enter the stadium
All the pre-match preparation out of the way.

As I enter through the gates
My body tingles
Hoping that one day I will be there.

As I take my seat
I can't wait for it to begin.

Finally the teams run out
And prepare to kick off.

As the ball leaves the kicker's boot
The tensions run as the players race for the ball
And as the opposition catch the ball.

I can't wait for the rest of the game
To be unravelled
With all its twists and turns

And I think to myself
What a wonderful game it is.

Oliver Newman (13)
Cirencester Kingshill School, Cirencester

Memories Of You

Memories of you are like a pool lit up by the sun,
The sun made out of crystals.
When I think of you,
My love is just for us and forever is a must.

Rachel Ody (13)
Cirencester Kingshill School, Cirencester

The Old House On The Hill

There is an old house,
Up on the hill,
It stands so weak, yet spooky and still.

It creaks whenever
A car rushes past,
No one knows
How long it will last.

Everyone that goes in,
Never comes out,
The only noises
Are the screams and shouts.

With its forgotten door,
Its contents unknown,
Abandoned is the house
Where no one goes.

They want to knock down
The house on the hill
And see what's inside,
But no one will.

There is such fear
Of the unknown,
The house on the hill,
So cold, so alone.

Katie Mackenzie (12)
Cirencester Kingshill School, Cirencester

The Harbour

The lime-green sea,
Washes up against the harbour wall,
The nice shiny yachts,
Float on the stagnant water,
The fish and crabs,
Swim and move,
In the brick-enclosed pool.

Behind the harbour,
Is the lush green grass,
And the stone brick shops
And bright colourful houses
That have white-framed windows,
That overlook
The magical sea.

The people rushing along the water's edge,
Looking for this year's bargain,
Buying ice creams and fishing nets,
Then, after a while,
They settle down on the harbour wall
With an ice cream in one hand
And a crab line in the other,
They sit and watch,
The glowing, red sun disappear over the horizon.

Isaac Herbert (12)
Cirencester Kingshill School, Cirencester

Bitching

Whisper, whisper, whisper
Laugh, laugh, laugh
They're at it again
The childish games they play
Just because they're bored
They feel the need to leave someone out
Mock what they say
Laugh behind their backs.

They think they're better than everyone else
They think they're untouchable
They need to feel important
Need to feel in control
But really
They're lonely
And insecure
The bitches are bitching.

Katrin Lager (13)
Cirencester Kingshill School, Cirencester

The Stormy Beach

The palm trees bend
The waves crash
The thunder roars
The village snores
The sky lights with rage
The thunder shatters my ears
The rain causes the sand to slip beneath my feet
Shadows flash upon the ground
The sky turned as grey as an elephant
All on this dark and stormy night.

Luke Barton (13)
Cirencester Kingshill School, Cirencester

Ferrets Are Sweet

F errets are sweet
E nergetic are they
R unning quickly
R apidly moving round his cage
E ating all the bugs that go past him
T om is his name
S miling always in his ferrety way!

A nd he's always cheeky
R ound his cage, wriggling out of small gaps
E thel is his sister - she is.

S oft as can be
W hite, fluffy fur
E ven though she never cleans herself!
E very time I walk past the cage, I think
T hey're the best ferrets in the world!

Jess Logan (12)
Cirencester Kingshill School, Cirencester

A Place Called Paradise

Another day in paradise
Comes to an end
The sun begins to set
The sky turns fire-red.
The sand beneath my toes starts to cool
The sea trickles further to the tips of my toes
A cool breeze whips the back of my neck
Then the sound of the ocean fades away
And the ringing of my alarm
Plays into my ear.
There's no more sand
Just my comfy duvet.

Jess Hollister (13)
Cirencester Kingshill School, Cirencester

Cristiano Ronaldo (Me)

Well, where do I start?
For one thing,
Look at me,
I was walking down the tunnel
In some style
And I brushed my teeth
So they were gleaming
And I got on my boots,
My lovely boots.

When I have that ball,
I run around them all,
Kicking that ball, is like
Kicking a teddy bear,
So soft, yet so gentle.

I thought I looked good in that pose,
From toes to nose,
Standing there with the ball at my feet,
Looking pretty sleek,
And when I run with my feet,
I look quite neat,
With the Man U kit on,
Wearing number seven.

With that stylish hair,
I was looking cool
And the expression on my face,
I looked like a fool.
We went on to win that match
And the League,
I can only say one thing,
AIG stands for Alex Is God
And I don't know about the photographer,
But I think he did a great job.

Joshua Baker (12)
Cirencester Kingshill School, Cirencester

Tiger Woods

The Tiger is proud, so proud,
The sound of the crowd, the crowd,
So much power, much power,
Rips through the air,
Three hundred yards in a second.

The Tiger is proud, so proud,
The sound of the crowd, the crowd,
So much power, much power,
Nike carries him along the way,
Tiger, top of the table.

The Tiger is proud, so proud,
The sound of the crowd, the crowd,
So much power, much power,
Above the great Monty,
Sand skills amazingly accurate,
Five strokes, done it in four.

James Bellringer (13)
Cirencester Kingshill School, Cirencester

Love

Love is a pink cloud floating in the mid summer sky.
Love is dark chocolate melting on your tongue.
Love is the sun setting on a winter's day.
Love is roses in a field of love.
Love is ice cream on a hot day.

Charlotte Williams (12)
Cirencester Kingshill School, Cirencester

The Nameless Creature

The nameless creature,
He stalks the sky,
With his huge feathered wings,
They beat the clouds,
Powering him along,
Faster, faster, faster.

The nameless creature,
He searches day and night,
Hunting down his prey,
Scouring the forests,
Skimming the lakes,
His eagle eyes watching.

The nameless creature,
He spots his prey,
He lands softly,
On his muscly limbs,
Creeping closer, closer,
Using his long tail to balance.

The nameless creature,
He leaps in the air,
Quickly and powerfully,
Grabbing his meal,
With his strong sharp talons,
The hunt is over.

The nameless creature,
Exhausted from flight,
Tears into the meat,
Crushing the bones while he feeds.
He takes a well-earned drink,
Then the hunt starts again.

Ben Mixture (13)
Cirencester Kingshill School, Cirencester

A Snowflake

I'm swooping,
I'm soaring in the sky,
I'm swirling,
I'm twirling down towards the ground,
What am I?

I'm small,
I'm dainty, like a fairy,
I'm magical,
And I'm always unique.
What am I?

I'm about to finish my flight,
I've landed,
I've finished my flight,
I'm crisp, I'm white,
I'm nice and snug and tight.
What am I?

There are lots of me,
Falling from the sky,
Swooping, soaring and twirling.
What am I?

Once we have landed,
We made a bed of white,
You use us
To build snowmen.
What am I?

We look like snow,
But we're not.
What am I?

I am a snowflake!

Laura Cox (12)
Cirencester Kingshill School, Cirencester

Friends

Friends are special,
Kind and sweet,
They keep secrets,
Like a treat.

They don't betray you,
They don't lie,
They're not traitors,
They don't make you cry.

They make you happy,
Make you laugh when you're sad,
They tackle your enemies,
Make them feel bad.

Friends are forever,
For always and true,
Never to end,
Like a never-ending clue.

Sapphire Rogers (12)
Cirencester Kingshill School, Cirencester

Pink Flower

Pink and pretty,
Its round petals,
My pink flower.

How beautiful it was,
Its lovely pink colour,
My pink flower.

Its petals all pink,
Sparkling for all to see,
My pink flower.

Kate Godwin (13)
Cirencester Kingshill School, Cirencester

Splish, Splash

Swaying and swerving,
Ducking and diving,
See this amazing creature,
Swimming round the ocean,
Round and round it goes,
Searching far and wide,
Looking for its prey,
The fish it likes to eat,
Deep down,
High up,
He keeps on searching,
Splish, splash,
Splish, splash,
The dolphin strikes,
Catching its prey,
In its mouth,
Nothing more,
Than a poor,
Innocent fish.

Charlotte Morris (13)
Cirencester Kingshill School, Cirencester

King Carlos

C arlos Tevez is his name
A ccording to me, he is the best
R ight wing is his position
L aughing off the opposition
O ffside is never his thing
S cores every shot

T aking on the players
E very single time
V ery expensive is his cost
E very shot hits the net
Z ooming past every player.
    Carlos Tevez.

Elliot Mace (11)
Cirencester Kingshill School, Cirencester

Best Friends

Friends, friends are together,
Friends, friends are forever,
When times are mad,
When times are sad,
You promise you will be there for me.

When people laugh at me,
I laugh back,
But if you were with me,
You would break their back.

You're always by my side,
To comfort me when I cry,
You are my best friend
And I'll love you till the end.

You make me smile when I am down,
You make me jump, I just frown,
When we fall out, my heart sinks,
You mean the world to me,
So just think,
Stay with me and be my best friend,
Like I told you, I will love you
Till the end!

Lauren Gleed (13)
Cirencester Kingshill School, Cirencester

Trees

Trees are tall and trees are small
Trees are thick and trees are thin
Trees make the world look beautiful
Trees make the world green.

Trees grow beautiful flowers from their buds
Trees make the world seem big and tall
They help the world by making oxygen
Drinking the world's greenhouse gases.

Ryan Curtis (12)
Cirencester Kingshill School, Cirencester

Ice Cube

Cold and chilling,
A touch of ice,
Freezing and frosty,
All day and night.

Silver sparkles all through the day,
Until the ice cube thaws away,
Cool and calming,
Splash into the drink,
Splishing and fizzing,
It gives you a wink.

Juicy red lips touching the cup,
The drink pours in,
And there's no slop,
The crunch of the ice cube,
The slurp of the Coke,
And then the person will go home.

Jake House (13)
Cirencester Kingshill School, Cirencester

Sunset Beach

S unlight rays
U nlike
N o other
S unshine leaving
E ventually going
T ime to say goodbye until the morning

B eautiful beach waves
E ating away
A t the golden beach sand
C limbing up the beach shore
H unting the dry sand.

George Jones (12)
Cirencester Kingshill School, Cirencester

The Dove Of Death

The dove of death
Evil
Flying above
Beams of light from the sky
A day of fire and death awaits.

A fiery boat flaming, smoky
Burning in the bright light
Screams of the dove of death
Death, death and death
More and more death every flame.

Waves crash onto the flaming embers
The flames die out, the boat sinks
Down, down, down
Down into the depths
Of the deep blue sea.

The dove of death.

Alex Lane (13)
Cirencester Kingshill School, Cirencester

Rafiki

I'm tall and hairy,
I live in a tree,
Where I sing and dance all day.
My name is Rafiki.

I may be a baboon, but I'm not stupid,
I bring guidance to young Simba,
Through his journey from young to old.

I'm loving and caring,
And all I really want
Is a big hug from you to me.

Chelsea Collins (12)
Cirencester Kingshill School, Cirencester

Snowy Mountains

A faint trickle of snowfall,
Lies gently on the ground.
A peaceful morning,
Everything so still, so quiet,
So calm.

The sky turns black with anger,
That peaceful morning is gone.
Clouds roll from east to west
And slowly the storm moves on.

Then the sun pokes its head out,
Over the mountainside.
Its rays beat down across
The snowy mountainside.
It slowly starts to disappear,
It's going . . . it's going . . . it's gone.

Jamie Gordon-Walker (13)
Cirencester Kingshill School, Cirencester

Fairy Magic

F airies come with lots of magic
A ll the fairies have a bag of fairy dust
I t only takes one minute each time
R unning out, not to worry
Y ell five times

M ajesty Lindear will give you more
A lot of rubbish, don't you think?
G rab it and throw it away type, well
I believe it
C an you?

Hannah Devine (11)
Cirencester Kingshill School, Cirencester

The Cricket Bat

I am a cricket bat,
Tall, long and proud.
I sit there in a case,
In a dark, dark cupboard.
I go out for practises,
I go out for matches,
I get dents,
I get scratches.
I break,
I get fixed,
Then I get chucked around,
I am broken again
At the end of the day.
Weeks,
Months,
Years,
I still manage to get fixed
And look as good as new.
I am the king of the cricket bats.

Paul Allen (13)
Cirencester Kingshill School, Cirencester

People All Around Us

P athetic people are bullies
E very day they bully people
O ne occasionally hits people
P lease, says the kid being bullied
L imping back to class, the bully pushes him
E veryone laughs when he falls over.

John Limb (12)
Cirencester Kingshill School, Cirencester

What A Big Place

What a big place
From the outside it looks tiny
As small as a mouse
But from the inside it's massive
Just like a normal house.

What a big place
It's all very scary
Everything twice my height
It's all a maze
It's such a sight.

What a big place
I've got used to it now
It's not as scary
It's not as big
But it's dark outside
And it's all so starry.

Katie Hobbs (13)
Cirencester Kingshill School, Cirencester

The Lonely Goat

The lonely goat
Sat in his boat
Travelling far and wide

He came to an island
What a lovely island
Travelling far and wide

He got some loving
Some red-hot loving
Travelling far and wide

Then he got some kids
Some loving kids
Travelling to work and back.

Luke Oosthuizen (13)
Cirencester Kingshill School, Cirencester

Mermaid On The Rocks

She was on the jagged rocks,
Brushing her long blonde locks,
Feeling quite appealing,
Looking over to the boats in the docks.

She dived into the sea blue
And didn't have a clue,
Swimming with the colourful fishes,
Coming up to the surface, the time was due.

The orange sun sets,
As all the boats pull in their fishing nets,
The fishermen see what they have caught,
Seeing all the fish,
Turn around, it's being served on a dish.

I get a glimpse of the white moon in the sky,
As an aeroplane goes by,
All the stars twinkle in my eye,
It's time to go now - bye!

Daniella Keen (12)
Cirencester Kingshill School, Cirencester

The Northern Lights

In the dead of night
The lights shine bright
Red, blue, green, colours all around
I stand and watch the Northern Lights.

The streams of colour are like a river forever flowing
All the colours are brightly glowing
Above my head the peaceful sight is growing
I stand and watch the Northern Lights.

As I head home the lights drop from the sky
I turn and say goodbye to the Northern Lights.

Thomas Woods (13)
Cirencester Kingshill School, Cirencester

The Sun

The sun rises in view
When the morning is due
But someone still sleeps
Is that someone you?

The sun is bright at midday
And you feel quite hot from the sun's burning ray
But use sun lotion to protect your skin
And enjoy the sun because you don't need to grin!

The sun will set and it will get less light
When it's crimson, golden, very colourful and bright
It goes down in the evening and it's gone by night
The sun has passed away and it's gone from sight.

It turns to night and the sun's not there
You can't see it, even if you stare
But don't worry, it will be back in the sky
No matter if tomorrow's wet or dry!

Tom Sargent (13)
Cirencester Kingshill School, Cirencester

The Polar Bear

The long and perfect white fur,
Swayed like long grass in a gentle breeze,
Her strong and powerful muscles
Rippled as she walked slowly and gracefully on,
Her huge paws thumping gently down,
Leave deep prints in the crisp white snow.

The polar bear walked on and on,
Back to her cubs waiting for food,
She can see the den,
Where her cubs lie waiting,
So she pushes on,
Through the blistering winds.

She greets her hungry cubs,
With a warm and welcoming hug
And in her mouth she carries a fish
Which she lays down on the flat snow
And she watches the young fluffy cubs
Eating before they sleep.

Stuart Evans (13)
Cirencester Kingshill School, Cirencester

The Waterfall

I'm quite large, but I come in all shapes and sizes
Sometimes thin, sometimes wide
Maybe tall and maybe small.

I make a splash onto anything in my way
I am blue and white
When birds see me they take flight.

I would end a river, but start one again
I see lots of views
Grass swaying
Trees tall
Oh, what fun it is to be a waterfall.

Rosie O'Connor (11)
Cirencester Kingshill School, Cirencester

The Sunset

The sun was slowly forced below the hills,
Fighting, reaching, desperate to see,
Crimson to violet, every imaginable hue,
Colliding with pinks, yellows - a rainbow of colour.
One final effort, begging to stay,
But the battle with night had been won.

Small, pricking sparks slowly appeared,
Piercing the sudden gloom which had
Replaced the warmth with heavy night.
The endless black silently pounced,
Dark, cold and unforgiving.

One streak of rich gold was all it took,
Breaking the blue with a ray of light.
The spell was broken for another day.

Jennifer Benton (13)
Cirencester Kingshill School, Cirencester

The Dragon And The Thing

As I stood there
Looking over the edge of the cliff
At the sunset
Which looked like nothing I'd seen before.

I was wondering why I was serving this thing sitting on me
While I could be roaming free on my own around the world
Is it my purpose in life
To be a slave

Or do I have another future
That awaits me?
Do you think I should
Leave this thing
And be free?

Marcus Rhodes (13)
Cirencester Kingshill School, Cirencester

Seeing And Growing

I stand here in a crowd,
But yet I still feel alone.
I am part of a group
And cannot move,
I feel the wind loop the loop.

The golden moon gleaming down,
From misted blue sky.
I stand on this hill,
I stare into mid-air, this is how I think,
I look over to the light-filled town.

My friends and family tower over
And why I do not know.
I asked the moon,
I asked the sky
And I was told that I will grow.

Siobhan Walker (13)
Cirencester Kingshill School, Cirencester

The Sun

The sun stays in the day and goes at night
It shines on the world day and night
Outside most of the time the sun shines all the time
Lying in the sun all day long, spend lots of time
Blazing hot, fiery heat, this is so hot you can feel the heat
Pressure on your body to keep the heat away
Killer heat burns so much, but doesn't keep
The heat never stops coming
The power of heat is unstoppable
And the heat is one of the worst things outside.

John Cornwell (13)
Cirencester Kingshill School, Cirencester

The Final Game

The day has come,
Where all fate will be decided,
The game is about to start.

I walked through the dark, hopeful tunnel
And entered the lush green stadium.
My heart was pounding and pulse racing,
The sound of fans chanting piled pressure
On the outcome of the game.

Then the National Anthem is sung,
Throughout the stadium the anthem is sung,
With their hands to their hearts,
Ready for the game of their lives,
It's up to us.

We get ready, put the ball down,
The whistle is blown, it has begun.
The day has come
Where all fate will be decided.
The game has started.

Jonathan Sampson (12)
Cirencester Kingshill School, Cirencester

Monkeys

M oving rapidly from tree to tree
O ver and under things in my path
N ever thinking twice about where I am
K eeping lookout for some prey
E nergetically through the jungle
Y et still not out of breath
S ettling down to eat some bananas.

Bethany Tindale (11)
Cirencester Kingshill School, Cirencester

Inhuman Menace

It gracefully glides over,
Frightening, intimidating, talking with its metallic voice.
With a plunger so deadly
And an unearthly weapon.
It feels hatred for everything,
Wanting to destroy and conquer.
Its eyestalk blue,
Looking you up and down.
It's come to a decision,
It's your end.
Nobody escapes the evil,
Of the Dalek.

Then a mysterious man,
Who calls himself the Doctor,
Appears from nowhere.
The Doctor, giving off almighty power,
Distracts the menace.
Your future is safe
And you escape,
Leaving the Doctor
With the Dalek,
'Exterminate!'

Andrew Hartnell (12)
Cirencester Kingshill School, Cirencester

Leopards

L eopards are spotty animals
E ating machines
O ver and under things
P ouncing on their prey
A gile animals
R ipping and eating meat
D isgracing others
S itting on the shady branches.

Lynn Kirkpatrick (12)
Cirencester Kingshill School, Cirencester

Castle

Standing there wondering
Standing there gazing
Standing there waiting

Bang, whizz, pop
Oh, ah
Sizzle, wizzle, sparkle
Oh, ah!

Watching the castle transform colours
Watching the twinkling fireworks
Watching the Tinkerbell as she jumps
Off the castle roof.

Screams of wonder
Shouts of happiness
Whistles of applause as Tinkerbell
Begins to land.

Nearly at the end
Nearly about to stop
But as it still goes on, so does the dream
But like all dreams, you have to awake
And realise it was just a dream or memory.

Jeanie Whelan (12)
Cirencester Kingshill School, Cirencester

Families

A family is people that stick together
Today and forever.
A family is people who help through the bad and good.
A family is people that give you pointers, through your life.
A family is people that love you today and forever.
A family is people that keep you safe.
A family is people that do things together forever.
That is what I think a family is.

Joshua Wall (12)
Cirencester Kingshill School, Cirencester

Cat's Eyes
(Inspired by L S Lowry)

Standing on the other side
Large green eyes see
The bleak, misty sky
Hung with billowing, black clouds of factory filth
Pale faces tear stained and scarred with permanent frowns
Enduring memories of war
Ironically reflected in lost limbs
Giant grey buildings oozing thick dark smoke
Like charcoal on white paper.

Standing on the other side
Delicate pointed ears hear
Hideous moans of pain
Cries of eternal distress
Distant church bells ringing emptiness
Like opportunities out of reach.

Standing on the other side
A small wet nose smells
The familiar scent of the matchmaker's labours
Phosphorus, spent fumes
Invading vulnerable lungs
Like a deadly bug waiting to kill.

Standing on the other side
A silky, slender feline feels
Cobbled, uneven ground
Beneath her elegant padded paws
Icy air numbing her to the bone
She senses desperate longing
For calm after the storm.

Grace Kinsey (12)
Cirencester Kingshill School, Cirencester

The Black Cat And The Tramp

The black cat
Prowls the street
Looking for mice and rats
To eat.

The outcast
Shunned by the crowd
He moves without a single sound
Climbs up a sail ship's mast.

The tramp
Sees the ship
Decides he should get out of the damp
Without meaning to, he takes a kip.

The ship starts to shudder
And leaves the dock
Not even hitting a single rock
With the aid of the captain controlling the rudder.

The cat no longer the outcast
Prowls the ship
Looking for mice and rats, as well as the odd food bit
And his home is now the mast.

The tramp no longer a tramp
Never has to shelter from the damp
And when he lies there on his bedding mat
He knows he has a friend; the black cat.

James Barry (13)
Cirencester Kingshill School, Cirencester

Criminal Mind

I'm in the wrong position,
To fuel my ambition,
I'm going to kill a politician,
With my aiming precision.

I've got a gun in my pocket,
I'm about to load it,
I'm walking down the street
And I feel the heat.

As a cop approaches,
My gun is loaded,
I shoot him to the floor,
And now he's no more.

I feel like a predator,
In the urban jungle,
The sky goes black,
Like a snooker eight ball.

When I speak,
I sound like a frog,
Croaking out words,
That have no meaning.

I have a criminal mind
And that's what you'll find.

Lewis Evans (12)
Cirencester Kingshill School, Cirencester

My Five Kittens

Beady eyes and titchy ears
Tiny tails and high-pitched squeals
Ginger, black, white and brown
Colours of my five kittens
Dotty, Patch, Gingey too,
Titchy, Stripe and mama Socks too.

Toni Mottram (13)
Cirencester Kingshill School, Cirencester

Badminton Horse Trials

The first one goes
Off at
The speed of light,
Everyone's eyes
Full of fear and fright,
Flying over the fence,
They look immense.
Commentator's voice
Full of delight,
The crowd hold
Their breath
At the sight.
A couple of miles
Or two,
The horses know what to do,
As they come
To the last fence,
The crowd blasts a cheer,
As they run
Through the finish line,
Knowing they're back
Where they started.

Megan Saunders (13)
Cirencester Kingshill School, Cirencester

Going On Holiday

Suitcase packed all ready to go.
Hope it's hot, I don't like snow.
On the plane eating my food,
I'm so excited, I'm in a good mood.

Off the plane, onto the bus,
To the hotel for all of us.
At the hotel and into the pool,
The sun is hot and the water is cool.

Emma Legg (12)
Cirencester Kingshill School, Cirencester

Stonehenge

Standing tall, above the world
Looming like a turret
Shadows dancing away from the sun
Impressive arches of stone

Slabs of rock, as grand as marble
Strong, like a pillar
Lived through thousands of passing years
With the wind whistling through

Full of memories, tales and secrets
Waiting to be told
Hiding in the cracks and corners
Weathered from centuries of rain

Standing tall, above the world
Looming like a turret
Shadows dancing away from the sun
Stonehenge in all its glory.

Abbie Ho (12)
Cirencester Kingshill School, Cirencester

Heartagram

H eartagram is when love and death collide
E veryone has seen it somewhere
A nd most have hated it
R eally it's Gothic
T hat's why I like it
A nyone can draw it, it's only a heart and a triangle, no
G ear is needed, just a pencil
R obert is my name
A nd as I said, I like it
M aybe because I'm slightly goth!

Robert Fowkes (11)
Cirencester Kingshill School, Cirencester

Grand Teton Mountains

The mountains, grand and superior,
Stretching high in the sky,
Where clouds sit motionless,
Like cotton wool.

The sky is a rich blue colour,
With the lake shimmering like sapphires in
The morning breeze,
Underneath it.

The mountains, snow-topped,
Stretching as far as the eye can see,
Then with a crunch,
And a splash,
Bits of it crumble into the lake,

Making it ripple into the horizon,
Just as the sunrise appears,
Clear and bright,
Ready to start a new day.

Nicole Brookes (12)
Cirencester Kingshill School, Cirencester

Eyes

Some are green,
Some are blue,
Some are brown,
They match the frown.

Everyone has their own,
Some old, some new,
They're all different in their own way,
But they are that special thing about you!

Abby Beasley (12)
Cirencester Kingshill School, Cirencester

Ghosts

They're white, they're scary
They're big, but not hairy
They scare big boys
And make them look like fairies.

They're your worst nightmares
They're even worse than bears
They make you stand on end
Especially your hairs.

You really must know
That my friend, Joe
Saw you in my room
That's why he screamed, *wooh!*

So remember, if you see a ghost
Be careful not to boast
You gotta watch out for the scare
So remember little kiddies, *beware!*

Tom Gardiner (13)
Cirencester Kingshill School, Cirencester

The Cat

The cat jumps up to the wall,
Along he goes,
Up the hill to the path,
He goes to the forest for some food,
Stalking his prey he goes,
He lies low and pounces,
The mouse is no more.
He goes up the tree for a rest,
In the morning he wakes,
He goes home for his food.

Elouise Ody (13)
Cirencester Kingshill School, Cirencester

The Day I Made My Teacher Disappear

I can remember that funny day,
The day my teacher went away.

A flash, a boom,
It shook the whole room,
The day she went away.

All I needed was the staffroom sink,
I didn't really need to think,
How she would go in a flash of pink.

The children all cheered when she was gone,
But unfortunately we were all wrong.
As we looked at her clothes on the classroom floor,
The whole class ran for the door,
Because she was back here once more.

She grew into a hungry beast
And she was looking for a feast.
So I ran into the canteen
And gave her a try of the gelatine.

There was a bang and a choke,
A big cloud of smoke
And now our teacher is gone.

Jodie Fletcher (12)
Cirencester Kingshill School, Cirencester

Romantic Scene

A romantic scene by the beach
I wonder what you see
The sun setting in the sky
Have a bit of apple pie
Maybe with a bit of ice cream
This would make a lovely dream

A romantic scene by the beach
I wonder what you'll get up to
Put on your swimming trunks
And have a little paddle
Or would you sunbathe
Near the warm, heavy sea?

A romantic scene by the beach
What would you do next?
How about a gorgeous scene
With maybe strawberries and cream?
Please do not have a nightmare
Or I would be in despair.

Dale Wall (13)
Cirencester Kingshill School, Cirencester

The Dreaded Haircut

When I'm at the hairdressers sitting on the chair,
I start to get fidgety as she cuts through my hair.
Going to the hairdressers is something I dread,
Because I worry the scissors will stick in my head.
I also worry they'll cut it too short,
Then I will look like a horrible dork.
The hairdresser starts a conversation about school,
Not something I like talking about as a rule.
It is now the end
And my hair is in the trend.

Laura Outram (13)
Cirencester Kingshill School, Cirencester

Deep, Deep Beneath

There I sit gazing into the sea,
Deep down lay a coral reef,
With a reflection of a handkerchief,
The fish swim down below,
But some fast and others slow,
With their shiny scales
And my painted nails,
I sit there gazing deep, deep beneath.

I sometimes think about being a fish,
When I see it being cooked in a dish,
What it would be like,
Would I be called Mike?
Could I swim as fast as a cheetah,
Or be a meat eater,
As I think,
I sit there gazing deep, deep beneath.

Amy Chinnock (13)
Cirencester Kingshill School, Cirencester

Looking For A Poem

So you want a poem?
Well, I could give you one,
Or maybe I will let you look at one.
Maybe poems are hard to find,
But I could give you one in the nick of time.
Fast or slow, I will give you one soon,
Or maybe you could have one of my tunes.
Poems are long or short in different ways,
They could even go on for a million days.
So you are still looking for one, well let me tell you,
I have just given you . . . a poem.

Oliver Lendon (13)
Cirencester Kingshill School, Cirencester

Memories

Memories are in the past,
Most of them never last,
Something happy, something sad,
Something good, something bad.

They make you smile, make you laugh,
Those crazy things that are ever so daft,
Could be anything or anyone,
Something you treasure but now it's gone.

Could be a friend, even a boy,
Or maybe just that simple cute baby boy,
Memories that are forever there,
Something you'll always share.

The cutest pet, or that romantic sunset,
A family member or that special day in December,
Memories are in the past,
They will last and last . . .

Carrie Bloodworth (13)
Cirencester Kingshill School, Cirencester

Skateboard

Skateboarding takes a lot of skills
Kick flip is a trick in skateboarding
A skateboard is made up from four wheels, wood and metal
To skateboard you need a lot of courage, skill and balance
Etnies is a make of a skating shoe
Best skateboarders win trophies
Ollie is a skateboard trick
A skateboard competition is held at a skate park
Deck is the top of the skateboard.

Bradley Robinson (13)
Cirencester Kingshill School, Cirencester

The World Of Ballet

Ballet is a magical thing,
It's elegant and graceful,
It's exciting and beautiful,
It's enchanting, it's pretty,
It's enjoyable.

Many people come and try,
The peaceful world of ballet,
Twirling and whirling,
Round and round,
Until they drop with dizziness.

Most everyone carry on,
For years and years to come,
But others quit or move away,
From the peaceful world of ballet.

Katie Moore (12)
Cirencester Kingshill School, Cirencester

Lilies

Lilies are beautiful flowers
dancing elegantly in the wind
their graceful petals fly through the sky.

With a beautiful fragrance of their own,
it would make a sweet perfume.
The petals are fragile like a wine glass
travelling across the sea.

Tuesday Townsend (12)
Cirencester Kingshill School, Cirencester

The Deserted Beach

Strolling down the calm, deserted beach,
I feel soft, silky sand passing through my feet
As I slowly sink into the golden sand.

As I sit hiding in the shade from the scorching sun,
The free-flowing turquoise sea
Was swashing around my ankles.

A parrot flashes past me,
Taking all its colours with it,
Stripes blue, stripes green, stripes yellow,
From a parrot circling around me.
I'm not alone on the beach as it's me and the sea.

Clare Wynn-Mackenzie (13)
Cirencester Kingshill School, Cirencester

Love

Love is like ripe-smelling roses on a warm spring day,
An uplifting feeling in your soul.
Love is a pink cloud of hearts
Showering you all over.
It's like chocolate melting in your mouth,
Like long Sunday lie-ins.
Love is like bubbles in fizzy drinks popping in your mouth.
It's as warm as a summer's day
And as fluffy and soft as a newborn bunny.
Love feels like a freshly made bed.
Love is as if fresh, calm, relaxing music is flowing all around you,
But most of all it's a unique feeling to you and I.

Rose Burston (12)
Cirencester Kingshill School, Cirencester

New School

All those kids were there inside,
When I came in and stood there awkwardly.
They had been laughing and joking,
But the class soon fell silent and eyes began to stare.
Then a faint whisper rippled through them,
Until it began to grow stronger.
'Who is she?'
And,
'Where's she come from?'
Echoed round and round.
It felt as if I was an alien from planet Pluto
And that thought made me feel worse than before.
Then the faintest form of friendliness came
It was in the form of a girl
She took my hand and introduced me.
She somehow softened the blow of questions
That the rest bombarded me with.

Two weeks went by . . .
All those kids were there inside,
When I arrived late and giggling.
They had been laughing and joking,
But now they included me in their laughter.
Me in their secrets
And
Me in their chatter.
I know that now I have made some friends,
However awkward it had seemed at first.

Caitlin McWilliams
Cotham School, Bristol

The Alien That Landed On Earth

All those humans staring at me
When I stepped down the iron spaceship stairs.
They were laughing, pointing, the people of Earth.
Boiling-hot Mars was my home planet,
So green was my skin; as green as wet copper.
My bright purple eyes hovered over my tiny head.
All ten looking for somebody comforting, kind.
But I stood, surrounded by horrible, scary earthlings.
1,000 people watching my every move,
Some poking my silver boots and gloves.
Dentists and doctors were inspecting me with drills,
All sorts of mechanical things.
Young children pulling at my wings.
It hurt like a bullet in my back.
My space suit was brand new, now it looked old
Because I'd been travelling through hot and through cold.
I was bruised and bashed from all the sticks and stones
Hitting my rough, bumpy skin.
I couldn't take it anymore so I got in my spaceship
Put on my metal shiny helmet, slammed the solid bronze door shut.
Soon I was speeding but still they went on.
One man took a picture, everyone copied.
I thought my problems were over, they've just begun.

Evie Miles
Cotham School, Bristol

I Had A Dream

I had a dream last night
Or should I say it was a nightmare
For in my dream, the Earth was not a planet
More like a living Hell.

The sky was black with toxic fumes
The sea was poisoned and polluted
The ice caps had melted long ago
And the rainforests were no more.

Thousands of animals had become extinct
Only a few survive
Hundreds of plants are dead as well
And the food chain is in pieces.

Then I woke up and turned on the bedside light
And then I turned it off again, as I realised it was not just a dream
It was the future - the future that we must prevent
I hope everybody else wakes up, before my dream becomes reality.

Tom Last (12)
Cotham School, Bristol

Darkest Corner

You sit alone in the darkest corner
Staring at the razor in your hand
What the hell is it
About yourself that you just can't seem to understand?

Now it is time
To retrace the line
For which has been abused too many a time before
Suddenly, the blood begins.

The scars do the talking
For which words just can't grip
So red and bulgy
It drips.

So pale and angry
You cry out in pain
Suddenly, you realise
You've lost too much
That you just can't regain.

Connel McLaughlin (13)
Cotham School, Bristol

Darkened Pit

The group of kids were sitting there,
They looked mean, one was eating a pear.
I opened the door, walked straight in,
I sat down, but sat on a pin.
'Stop!' I yelled, 'That's very mean!'
They didn't reply, they didn't seem keen.

Why? I thought, *why do it to me?*
They stared in my eyes and said, 'Don't you see?
You're different from us, you will always be.
Don't deny it, go back across the sea.'

The guy with the pear was holding the core,
He threw it at me, he didn't want it anymore.
They laughed and laughed,
They pointed and screamed,
I didn't want to go on, but they worked as a team.
I sat in the corner getting punched and hit,
Then I disappeared into the darkened pit.

Kate Brennan (12)
Cotham School, Bristol

They Flew

They flew above me.
I could never reach them.
They dipped and soared,
I tripped and wobbled.
I wished I had wings,
Me, the little, wingless hedgehog.
They chirped at me
In what seemed like mocking voices.
They circled me and then swooped away.
The wind ruffled my spiky prongs,
Instead of making me airborne.
Me and my brown fur,
Them and their colourful plumage.
They came down towards me.
I pawed the air in hope,
But they just pecked me and flew and flew,
Until they were tiny specks in the distance.
So I curled up and slept.
Alone.

Jake Thompson (12)
Cotham School, Bristol

The Sky

Imagine if you could fly away,
In the clouds your mind would play,
Nothing that you could not say
And flying free every day.

Even if you cannot see
And you do not feel free,
The light will be the key,
Freedom comes, I decree.

And though it may seem a sin,
To not keep those feelings in,
To do that stabs like a pin,
So trust me and trust your kin.

The stars will guide you in the night
And they will help you with your sight
And provide you a lot of light,
For they will help you with this fight.

So hurry and rush through the sky,
Never listen to those who lie,
Better hurry, the end is nigh,
So watch out now, or you will die.

Thomas Jenkins (15)
Cotham School, Bristol

So What?

All those party poopers chatting and dancing.
I came in wearing jeans and a boring T-shirt.
My matted hair was tied tightly in bunches.
Everyone else was pointing and glancing.
So what if I hadn't come as a glitzy celeb!
All their eyes glittering like disco balls.
Staring at me like I was some kind of fool.
A girl came up to me and looked me up and down.
So what if I wasn't like them!
They all fell back laughing, calling me 'clown'.
My eyes throbbed, tears streamed down my face like the rays of blue
From the party light above.
So what? I don't care!
This was enough for me, I strolled down the street.
My feet making thuds like the beat of the music.

Josie Brown
Cotham School, Bristol

A Picture Paints . . .

Piercing winged arrows
Dart beneath the lazy currents
They slip through the rolling waves
And avoid the majestic manta rays;
Which skim the sandy ocean floor
And fill the coral reef galore!

The darting birds fill their beaks
The captured fish are lined with streaks
Sandy storms swirl about
Whipping stardust in and out
A sandy nebula starts to form
An entire galaxy has been born!

Inside a rotting fishing vessel
Splendid fish and crabs are nestled
In this varied underworld
A vibrant city is unfurled.

Nick Henden (15)
Culverhay School, Bath

Living On The Edge

I try to shout, as I scrape on the walls,
But my dodgy tunes fade me out,
My hard exterior is nothing compared,
To how I feel right now.

People move and hit me,
The electricity drives me insane,
They're so good at pressing my buttons,
But I've no time to make a fuss.

The same four walls always surround me,
I feel used and depressed,
Working hard day and night,
But never recognised for my work.

I'm always working to get to the next level,
Raise my game,
My PB an ETA,
Striving to be number one.

Never let free,
Never applauded
And as they go bankrupt,
Never to be seen again.

James Eynon (14)
Culverhay School, Bath

The Killer Machine

The four metal solid walls
Metal roof, metal floor
Lush, soft blue carpet
Luminous strips of light shining above
Walls covered with glass
Small room, seems much bigger
Stopping at random levels
People jump on
People jump off
Soon it begins to strain
Creaking
Worried glances
Then it snaps!
Falling fast!
Their lives flash before them
Screaming! Panic!
The crash!
The lift explodes!
Their lives are over
The killer machine is born!

Peter Calley (14)
Culverhay School, Bath

I'm Not A Yo-Yo

I only stop
When they run out

When they run out
They come back as more

My life's always in danger
But I keep holding on
By the hair on my head

There isn't much of it
But enough for what's required

Over the years, I've got stronger
As strength is needed for my struggle against death.

Joe Payne (14)
Culverhay School, Bath

The Trials And Tribulations Of School

There goes the bell for period one
Then you know the school day has just begun
I come to school to see my mates and to learn
But all my enemies want is for the school to burn

Once again lesson two is Hell
Thankfully, there goes the bell
Break time, a detention for the class
An aeroplane's thrown, no one likes a grass

So little time, too much work
To me the bad person is just a jerk
English, French, too much to take in
Oh look, it's his birthday, time for the bin

That's the trials and tribulations of school
I want to be a teacher, people say, 'What a fool!'
To do that, I've got to learn
One day it will be *my* kids turn.

Paul Yearley (13)
Lakers School, Coleford

Imagine

I f I were older
M y wish would be to sing
A nd learn how to be a singer
G etting better every day
I n each and every way
N o turning back
E njoying my life.

Mirelle Cross-Jones & Georgina Turton (14)
Rowdeford School, Devizes

Imagine

I f I were a world champion
M y sport would be basketball
A gainst all opponents
G etting good as I go
I n the game scoring, scoring, scoring
N BA Championship games
E nding with my team with the cup.

William Filer (15)
Rowdeford School, Devizes

Imagine

I f I were a
M ighty expert on
A   dinosaur that I know, a
G igantic dinosaur
I would tell everyone
N ew and interesting things about it
E den, excellent speech!

Eden Saunders (15)
Rowdeford School, Devizes

Imagine

I f I were a
M illionaire
A ll the money
G reed
I wanted
N ever shared
E veryone envious.

Craig Lundberg (15)
Rowdeford School, Devizes

Growing Up

When I was born I was named Holly
And I was known to be very jolly
When I went to school
I had lots of friends
We went on a school trip and saw lots of hens
When I was in Year 6
We had a leaving party
And all of us practised karate
First day at seniors, it all went great
But some of the teachers I really hate
It's time to go now
I've had lots of fun
And those are all the things
In my life I've done.

Hannah Landon-Hammond (12)
St Benedict's Catholic Sports College, Cheltenham

Growing Up

When I was one
I learnt how to kick a ball
And to suck my thumb.
Then I was two
I got bigger
So I needed clothes that were new.
Then I was three and four
I went to playschool
It was horrible
And thought it wasn't cool.
Then I got to five
I went to infant school
I got another new ball.
Then I was six, seven, eight and nine
I looked after anything that was mine.
Then I got to a two digit number
Which was ten,
I was getting closer to being
One of the men.
Then I was eleven, twelve and thirteen
And I got to be really mean.
Then I got to fourteen, fifteen and sixteen
And my voice broke
And finally I turned into a bloke.
After I was seventeen and eighteen
I got old enough to drink
I would start to have hangovers
And not know what to think.
Then I got to twenty-three
I got married and had a son
Just after one year of age
He knew how to run.
I had a great life
Still playing for a football team
That was my dream!

Cameron Smith (12)
St Benedict's Catholic Sports College, Cheltenham

Growing Up

Four years old and starting school
Being yourself, not acting cool
Always nice and making friends
Never wanting the day to end

Going out and having fun
Playing with mates in the sun
My life's so perfect, it truly is
But people say it's cos we're kids

Eight years old, turning mature
Still getting jealous, looking for a cure
Becoming nervous by tests and SATs
Fighting with siblings, calling them brats

Twelve years old and everything's changing
Personality, style and my body's aging
With the years going by, getting older
My heart's gradually getting colder

Fighting with enemies, about to lie
Life's getting hard, starting to cry
Who can help? What do I do?
No longer have friends who are true

Feeling like everyone's against me
Needing help and TLC
I ask myself, 'Why is life so tough?'
I guess it's just growing up!

Lauren Randell (12)
St Benedict's Catholic Sports College, Cheltenham

Growing Up

I'm a seed growing big
I'm in the ground with soil on my head
Now the water is poured on me
Now I'm sprouting, growing big.

I'm starting to come out of the ground
I use the light to make my food
The food gives me energy to grow up tall
Now I'm blossoming.

Soon the leaves will come
Then my tree will be as big as the rest
Roots growing down
Me growing up.

Now I'm growing apples
Maybe I'm an apple tree
Giving fruit to whoever owns me
Giving them lots of goodness.

Tanya Tucker
St Benedict's Catholic Sports College, Cheltenham

When I Grow Up

When I grow up, I want to be a teacher
So I can teach all of the children what to do
But I don't want to have to take them to the loo
I would love to work in a nursery with little children
I love seeing little children be happy
But I don't like their smelly nappies
After all the children have finished their lunch
We put them to bed by patting their head
When it's time to go home
We say goodbye
And we're all alone.

Charlotte Davies (13)
St Benedict's Catholic Sports College, Cheltenham

I'm Growing Up

I'm growing up tall and strong,
But so full of emotion, proud and blue.

My tears are a tiny river of sadness,
Falling from my eyes.

My smile is like a ray of light,
Coming from my heart.

My heart is full of hope, anger
Sadness and pain.

All torn into pieces
Not knowing what to do.

Now I'm growing up, everything has changed,
I've made new friends, but lost old friends.

But there is one thing that has not changed,
My love for my family, which stands tall and firm.

Elizabeth Hart (12)
St Benedict's Catholic Sports College, Cheltenham

Growing Up

Growing up is like a flower
It's an extraordinary power
First of all, it's like a seed
When you start your years of need
Then you spot the very first leaf
And you start to grow some teeth
Some time later you'll see some petals
And you'll be winning lots of medals
The flower will soon attract bees
As you fly overseas
Finally it's a fully grown flower
You are too and you have the power.

Scott Boon
St Benedict's Catholic Sports College, Cheltenham

Growing Up

Growing up is very tough,
All the fight can be very rough,
Tears of happiness of all the class,
Because that big, fat bully has fallen to the grass!

Children playing all around,
Parents shouting up and down.

Teenage run always run away from home
Left under that bridge, or on the side of the road alone.

Friendships making,
Friendships breaking,
Fashion changing,
People aging.

When I was young, I was mad
But now I am older, I would say I am rad!

I used to think jelly shoes were cool
If you wear them now, you're a complete fool!

I used to collect McDonald's toys,
Used to moan when they gave you the Action Man for boys.

Sleeping at other friends' houses
Trying to be as quiet as a mouse
Otherwise
Mum and Dad will go mad
And be very sad
Because they couldn't get to sleep last night
So now they are having a fight.

Soon to be married and having babies,
They're all popping up like daisies.

Life passes so quick
It will be all over in a tick.

So make the most of what you have
And be grateful and have a laugh!

Michaella Rayson
St Benedict's Catholic Sports College, Cheltenham

Growing Up!

Growing up in Cheltenham Town,
Only Ward is fit for the crown!
The money I get is always in pence,
What would we do without you, Spence?

Education at St Benedict's is what we're havin',
At the back we have Gavin!
To survive in school you need goodwill,
We can always rely on you, Gill!

We don't have much, just random stuff,
A solid defender has got to be Duff!
All around me, I'm surrounded by pigs,
Number one goalie has got to be Higgs!

Lives aren't usually this sturdy,
But we'll always have you, Birdy!
How I've done well, I need to know how,
On the wings we have Yao!

Some days you might have downers,
Good to see you're with us Towners!
What I've learnt is we're all winners
Good job we have you, Finners!

Sam Morgan (14)
St Benedict's Catholic Sports College, Cheltenham

Growing Up

Growing up, whizzed around Earth,
Sometimes happy, sometimes sad,
Sometimes angry, sometimes joyful,
But never a word he spoke.

Growing up, stormed his way around the world,
Breaking things and crushing things,
Making people shout,
You never know when you might catch him,
Leaving disaster behind him
And his colour was red!

Growing up, skipped his way around,
Making people laugh and learn
In his eyes was joy
And his colour was blue.

Kyle Smith
St Benedict's Catholic Sports College, Cheltenham

Growing Up!

When I was small
I wished I were tall
When I was able to walk
I was able to talk
When I was at school
I looked a real fool
When I was weak
I got called a geek
When I was in secondary school
I almost killed my teacher with a tool
When I had my first C3
My mum slapped me.

Dylan Pezzack
St Benedict's Catholic Sports College, Cheltenham

Growing Up

When you're a baby
You crawl and whine
But all your dad does
It drink lots of wine.

Once you're three
You go to nursery
And grow more teeth
And you get big feet.

Two more birthdays
You'll be five
You start to go to school
You learn words like 'hive'.

A few more years
You're in secondary school
Where you will make new friends
And go to the swimming pool.

When you're an adult
You see less of your parents
But deep down inside
You love them, no matter what.

Liam Powell (12)
St Benedict's Catholic Sports College, Cheltenham

Growing Up

Life is like a roller coaster
It has its ups and downs
When you're happy or sad
If you're excited or angry
Life is like a roller coaster.

Alistair Potter (12)
St Benedict's Catholic Sports College, Cheltenham

Growing Up
(Based on 'The Sound Collector' by Roger McGough)

'A stranger called this morning
Dressed in black and grey
Put every sound into a bag
And carried them away'

The crying of a baby
The yawning of the parents
The squeaking of the pushchair
The sighing of the big brother

The tapping of the footsteps
The calling of the mum
The light snoring of the baby when it's asleep
The burping of the baby after it just ate

The flickering of birthday candles
Then blowing at the candles to blow them out
The *yes!* at the first pair of high heels
The *brumming* of the first set of wheels.

Claire Grey (12)
St Benedict's Catholic Sports College, Cheltenham

Growing Up

When I was one
My mum got me Thomas the Tank Engine
When I was two
I started to walk
When I was three
My brother was born
When I was four
I moved to Cheltenham
When I was five
I first watched TV.

Callum Brooks
St Benedict's Catholic Sports College, Cheltenham

Growing Up

My eyes opened this morning at four,
The first thing I saw was my bedroom door.
My mum made me breakfast and taught me to eat,
When I was two, I counted to ten on my feet.
When I was five, I started school,
Some kids there were really cool.
My teacher taught me how to write
And how to stay out of a fight.

When I was seven, I first rode a bike,
It felt so much better than my babyish trike.
When I was nine my dad taught me to make money,
I thought he looked really funny.
Now I'm twelve, I've got a mobile phone,
Its constant ringing makes my parents groan.
When I grow up I want a car
And have the best career by far.

Joe Horsted (12)
St Benedict's Catholic Sports College, Cheltenham

Growing Up

When I was one
I used to suck my thumb
And be hugged a lot
People used to squeeze me
Like I was a teddy bear
That has been handed down
From generation to generation
Now I am twelve
I am eleven years older
I am capable of what I am doing
My mum treats me thus
And here endeth my poem.

Charlotte Randall (12)
St Benedict's Catholic Sports College, Cheltenham

Growing Up And Growing Old

Growing up and growing old
I don't want to be bald
All my toys and all my things
Laying there in the bin

Growing up and growing old
I don't want to be bald
Moving school leaving friends
I don't think I'll be as sad again

Growing up and growing old
I don't want to be bald
It's so big, I'll get lost
Look at the time, I'm late
Now I'm ready to leave

Growing up and growing old
I don't want to be bald
End of school
End of hard work
Time to start having fun
Here come the tears again
Leaving school and growing up

Growing up and growing old
I don't want to be bald
Life is hard
Life is grim
I want to be a child again

Growing up and growing old
I don't want to be bald
My worst nightmare, how can it be?
I've turned *bald!*
Now I know why they say I wish I was a kid

Growing up and growing old
Why am I bald?
Growing old

Nearing the end
Life has been swell
But now I know life's coming to an end
As my heart stops, as I close my eyes
My life flashes before me
The good times and bad
And I die a happy man.

Stephen Oldroyd (11)
St Benedict's Catholic Sports College, Cheltenham

Growing Up

Paths we make,
Choices we make,
Paths we take alone,
Choices we make on our own!

I used to call her Mummy,
But now it is just Mum!

From a baby,
We must grow,
To a toddler,
Off we go!

I am going on thirteen,
Twenty-one as people say,
As they watch me,
Grow each day.

Now I am nearly thirteen,
What a lifetime is has been,
From the good to the bad,
The happy and the sad!

Lauren Quemby (12)
St Benedict's Catholic Sports College, Cheltenham

Walk Alone

Paths we take
Choices we make
Paths we take alone
Choices we make on our own

We all grow up and learn
We all take different turns
Turns in our path of life
Turns that may lead to strife

Problems we go through
Problems exists in other lives too
Having problems are not wrong
Having problems do not stay forever long

Conflict causes growth in many ways
Lessons we learn will always stay
Conflicts we gain as years go on
Lessons we learn, make us more strong.

Aaron Walker (12)
St Benedict's Catholic Sports College, Cheltenham

Growing Up

I've developed from a tiny seed
Into the world I've come
My mum and dad are pleased.
A baby boy, a bundle of fun
I am their newborn baby son.
Birthdays come and go each year
As well as Christmas full of cheer.
My life so far, has been such joy
Now I'm growing into a fine young boy.
Football and rugby mad, that's me
Drives Mum mad but she still loves me!

Ryan Pearce-Smith (11)
St Benedict's Catholic Sports College, Cheltenham

Growing Up!

First you're small
Then you get tall
Some of us are pains
And some are saints!

When you're a baby
Your cries are ear burning
Then you start to mumble
But at least your are learning.

Before you know it, you're years older
And you start your new school
You make lots of friends, some maybe taller
Some of them are cool and some maybe fools.

After your primary school, you start secondary
Which where I am now,
There are much more annoying teenagers
And the rest of their behaviour, I do not wish to tell!

Emma Stephens
St Benedict's Catholic Sports College, Cheltenham

Growing Up

When I was little, I didn't want to grow up
I saw my brothers and sister
They had spots and were smelly
They said school was fun
But I wanted to stay home with Mummy and Daddy
The boys and girls at school looked scary
And some of the teachers were real lairy
I made a friend, we still are now
I'm glad now, that I grew up.

Rebekah Swain (13)
St Benedict's Catholic Sports College, Cheltenham

Growing Up!

Growing up is really cool,
'Cause you don't go to school,
Growing up is really cool,
'Cause you can follow a whole new rule.
Growing up is also bad,
'Cause full time jobs, bills to pay,
Only four weeks holiday!
Growing up is really cool,
Driving cars by shore.
Growing up is really cool,
Owning an Olympic swimming pool.
Growing up is really cool,
Going on a date with Justin Timberlake.
Growing up is also bad,
Listing to your children's taste in music,
Oh, how sad.

Megan Davis
St Benedict's Catholic Sports College, Cheltenham

Poem

What do I want to do when I grow up?
One thing's for sure,
I do not want to be lazy and live off the state
I dream of a life that has fortune and will be great!

I'd love to work with cars
And enjoy spending time with my mates
In clubs and bars.

I hope to find the love of my life
Who will eventually be my wife.

How many children we will have
I don't know?

All I want is for us to be happy
And watch them all grow.

Aaron Pearce (12)
St Benedict's Catholic Sports College, Cheltenham

Growing Up

Growing up is fast
And a lot changes in
That period of time in
Your life.

You need to learn
You need to cry
You need to eat
You need to drink
You need to swim
All to
Get away from bad.

You need to give money
To charity to help the poor
To maybe give them a plate
Of food each day of the week.

You need to stop the bad and
Help the poor.

Give your respect to others
And help each other in your
Own way . . .

Growing up is fast
A lot of changes in
That period of time in your life.

Kim Rayner (12)
St Benedict's Catholic Sports College, Cheltenham

Growing Up

At first I was the little one,
A baby so wriggly and pink,
People used to coo like pigeons,
They don't anymore, I think.

Then I learnt to walk
And speech I did gain,
I started making random words,
It really was a pain.

I got older again
And with a *whoosh!* The years went past,
Finally, I was four
And I started school at last.

I learnt many things,
Like how to read and write,
I also learnt times tables,
When I got over the fright.

I was trusted more and more,
My mum let me keep pets,
The real problem came,
When they needed to see the vet.

And then the time came,
For me to change school,
I moved up to St Benedict's,
Where me and my friends rule.

So that is what happened,
The beginning, middle and end,
I hope for a good future
And I hope any breaks I will mend.

Tessa Dainty (12)
St Benedict's Catholic Sports College, Cheltenham

Younger

I was looking through pictures of my mum
When she was young
When I said to my mum,
'Who is this? Is it me when I was young?'
And she said no.

The last time I had a bottle
Was when I was young
The last time my mum had baby food
Was when she was young.

The last time I had a dummy
What when I was young
The last time my mum sucked her thumb
Was when she was young.

The last time I was scared
Was when I was young
The last time my mum was scared
Was of a spider when she was young.

The last time I blew bubbles
Was when I was young
The last time my mum watched Bagpuss
Was when she was young.

The last time I was young.

Abby Martin
St Benedict's Catholic Sports College, Cheltenham

Growing Up!

When I was born, I cried a lot,
But when I was a baby I nap a lot.

Two little eyes
Discovering what's new
Two little hands
Touching everything in view
A sweet little voice
Asking you why
A mischievous smile
Two little feet
Jumping on the floor
A toddler's mission
Is to explore.

As I'm continuously growing up
My mission is to learn from my mistakes.
One, two, three, I learn how to count,
Four, five, six, I learn how to read,
Seven, eight, nine, I learn how to draw,
Ten, that's what I am now.

Now school, school, school, is the resolution in education
School is the source to succeed
Learn; learn, I need to learn, not chat in the class.
Listen to my teacher and I will learn
End of school I will be surprised
I'm moving to the next year!

Marinel Kristine Jocson
St Benedict's Catholic Sports College, Cheltenham

Changing Schools

Changing schools is scary, because you don't know what's to come
Not learning, just watching films in the last week of term
Then comes a day when the whole class goes out
We went for a limo ride round a roundabout
Then we went on a trip, the class and I, we went to PG1
Then there's the day where we have to go
The day that I couldn't wait for.

Here I am at secondary school, everything's OK
Work's not hard at all
I've made some friends called Adam and James
As I get farther in the year, the work is getting harder
Now I wish I was back at primary school
Missing all my old friends
I go upstairs to go to my class
And some Year 11s push me back down
Now I'm in Year 11 getting ready for my tests.

I've got a good grade and a really good job
Just met a girlfriend going out tonight
We've arranged a date for the wedding
It's a big surprise . . .

Michael Davis
St Benedict's Catholic Sports College, Cheltenham

Growing Up

Can you remember when you were little . . .
Just running around having fun.
But now we are growing up
And it's time to let the new generation have a turn.

Can you remember when it was cool
To wear white socks pulled up!
Or getting so happy over something so small
Like writing with a pen at school
How about when the Spice Girls were cool
Or going to McDonald's just for the toys
And when Fresh Prince of Bel-Air was the best.

Can you remember what it was like
Just to have fun
Without anyone saying anything?
Or when Bubblegum Club was the coolest site.

But now running around isn't cool
And football socks have taken over
And at school, what's all you can write with, a pen
Spice Girls have been replaced by other groups
And a 'Happy Meal' wouldn't fill us up!

Julia White (13)
St Benedict's Catholic Sports College, Cheltenham

Growing Up

My mum said I was a good baby
And slept the whole night through,
I loved all of the attention I got from friends and family,
Cuddled and loved by all who knew me
This made me happy too,
I grew each day, getting bigger and bigger
As now it's clear to see.

My toddler years faced challenges and risks
That I would take,
I'd run and use my energy and fall all of the time,
I never listened to my dad
When he said watch that lake,
I would just run and catch the ducks
And think that they were mine.

I soon grew up and now a young boy
I watch others around me,
I've learnt from life and realise
That I was a normal toddler,
Although I am still young, I know how hard I used to be,
I will, from now on, listen to my parents each day as I get older.

Jordan Randall (13)
St Benedict's Catholic Sports College, Cheltenham

Being Young

I hate being young
People don't think you can do anything
You don't know any better though
All you want to do is sleep and have fun
They just won't leave you alone

Friends are part of growing up
Friends are growing just like you
They are young and don't know any better
They want to be left alone to have fun too

When I'm older though
I'll be the best
I'll be able to do anything
Then they'll leave me alone

See? I can be smart too
I can do what I want, where I want
But then I'll see some kids acting different
And start to nag them about the way they should be.

Lindsay Waters (13)
St Benedict's Catholic Sports College, Cheltenham

What Will It Be Like?

I'm going to secondary school!
But what will it be like?
I have buzzing questions in my mind that finally settle with
a wallop, crash, bang
I've seen stuff on TV
It looks as dull as watching rain
But it looks as scary as the monsters under my bed
And those big-eyed ones in my cupboard.

Anyway all this secondary school business is making me scared
And if only I cared
I might not dare
To go into this place full of monsters
And big people towering over us.

But now I'm here and let me tell you it's brill!
Oh sorry can't chat, got to go to English, it's my favourite subject.
It's the heart of the school!

Dipika Patel
St Benedict's Catholic Sports College, Cheltenham

Turn Back Time

Sitting in a room, looking backward
Over one shoulder. Seeing what is not
Visible through your memory. Remembering
Chances slip away through your fingers
With slow deliberation. Like catching smoke
With your bare hands; or catching the wind. You can't
Stop remembering. Hopeless, but addictive.

Questions answered wrongly; and answers
That were not given at all. The wrong word,
Giving another false hope, only to dash it. A step
Back, to give another a chance to fill my shoes.
Only to find out she does it better than me. Settling
To be a loser, to come second place. Just to save
The bother of fighting for something that was worth fighting for.

You turn back the time; put back the hands
Of the clocks. Blindly retrace your steps; backwards,
Trusting. Then take the right turning down the road.
Repair the error of your judgement. Say, 'yes'
Instead of, 'no'. Then stubbornly refuse to be
The martyr that you were the first time. Fight
For something worth fighting for.

But that was then; this is now. This white dress
On the bed is not yours. The church bells do not
Ring for you; the joy is not for you. Neither
Is the man downstairs. You only have lost chances,
Haunting memories and total abandonment. You
Learn not to turn back time; you only have the future.
You smile and try not to cry.

Hannah Shearer (15)
South Wilts Grammar School for Girls, Salisbury

A World Apart

You don't understand what it's like to be me
My world has more potholes than you care to see
'You can't really know them,' your answer replies
When you find out I'm talking to strangers online
Technology is changing and you're quick to judge
You're set in your old ways and won't care to budge.

You don't understand what it's like to be me
How listening to music sets all my stress free
It may not sound 'pleasing' but lyrics come first
You scream at me daily, 'Your eardrums will burst!'
These lyrics they run deep and echo in my mind
They give me the answers that I cannot find.

You don't understand what it's like to be me
Why in our conversations I never agree
Your mind is one-tracked, set for the past
You need to open your mind and see it at last
Things which you assumed made me so mad
Like it was no fault of your own that I acted so 'bad'.

You don't understand what it's like to be me
Why sometimes I just need to stare out to sea
If we take life too serious, we'll get too bogged down
We need an escape route - a place out of town
That's why I use my imagination and dream a new place
Where I can be who I want to be, without changing face.

Rachel Warne (17)
South Wilts Grammar School for Girls, Salisbury

Monday Morning

Sitting in English, uninspired,
I look at the clock, worn out and tired,
Trying to think of a poem to write,
I desperately try to look for the light.

For the weekend had been eventful,
A little resentful,
Stuffed with coursework and no play,
I wish these A levels would just go away.

Then comes Monday morning
And without warning
My friend explodes like a buddy balloon
Looking like a great buffoon.

To make matters worse,
I'm totally cursed,
I forgot to fill out a pink slip,
The teacher shrieks, 'Get a grip!'

So, I really hope,
So, I will cope,
The canteen has some good grease,
Cos I just wanna get obese!

Imogen Copp (16)
South Wilts Grammar School for Girls, Salisbury

Untitled

I've never felt so scared
Just walking through a shop door
The doorframe towers over me
Intimidating and foreboding

My feet move reluctantly
I have to concentrate
Putting one foot in front of the other
I glance behind me

They are all stood there
Watching me
I feel their gazes burning through me
I slowly walk further into the shop

I know they can't see me now
I can't do it
I won't do it
How can I get out?

My body screams to be on autopilot
My brain is screaming at me to stop
My body carries on moving
I am standing in front of the health drugs.

Anna MacDiarmid (16)
South Wilts Grammar School for Girls, Salisbury

Three Star Hotel

A woman in a cocktail dress, sits waiting in the lobby,
Jewels hanging from her like droplets
Falling off an elegant ice sculpture.
A man in a 70s styled suit comes ambling into the lobby
And stands in the corner,
Making eye contact, he beckons her towards him.

                        In a modern-styled apartment, sits a woman,
                    She seems around 30, but is dressed rather maturely.
              Clutching tightly onto an oblong box and a bottle, she stands
              And walks across the room, turns and looks out of her window.

The cocktail dress, now cast to the corner of a three-star room,
Lies crumpled and rejected like an unwanted rag.
The suit, folded nicely however, is lying on the table,
A plain gold wedding ring is flung across the room at great speed.

                The box, now open, has exposed a rather gleaming object.
                          Clasped tightly by the woman,
                    Her wedding ring removed and thrown into the corner,
                                  She sips from the bottle.

The man, tired, red and a thousand pounds down stands,
He edges towards the window and looks across the street.

                      A shot, a crime, a murder,
                      An affair.

A women in a cocktail dress stands in a room,
Blood hanging from her like droplets
Falling off an elegant ice sculpture.
A man in a 70s styled suit lies dead on the floor,
Eyes closed, she edges away.

                          In a modern styled apartment, sits a woman,
                    She seems around 30, but is dressed rather maturely.

Clutching tightly onto a gun and an empty bottle, she stands,
And walks across the room, turns and looks out of the window.

A new woman . . .
A new widow!

Paige Christie (15)
South Wilts Grammar School for Girls, Salisbury

Reminiscence

A long time ago I looked across this loch.
Memories. Water. The lonely sparrow.
Sweet words had caressed his tongue,
Embracing my heart in a world of hope.
A tune of such tenderness, had spoken to me,
A touch so soft, had embraced me.
Under the stars we'd lain,
Talking of our future; a new life.

Happiness filled my world,
A wedding dress so divine,
A groom so pulchritudinous, sublime.
The wedding ring upon my finger
Recalled faith to my mind;
I'd learnt to love again.
And what a joy this was to find,
When I finally knew I'd feel no pain.

How looks can be deceiving,
I thought I knew him so well.
Grief entwined my enraged heart,
While I sit here and remember.
The water that laps against the shore,
The lonely bird that calls;
An eternal cycle, unlike that of love,
But yet, his bitter devotion that lacerated my heart.

Iona MacDonald (15)
South Wilts Grammar School for Girls, Salisbury

The Argument

The very epitome of my frustration:
An arid landscape
Drowning in irony
Cool against my frozen fingers
Untouchable
Unbreakable
Unwanted

Sentences choke and diminish within my throat
Right words come and fade
Nothing but old clichés
To despair those vacant remains
Meaningless
Pointless
Loveless

Flotsam and jetsam, a suitable travesty
But the glue won't hold
And the mask is slipping
Revealing a furrowed brow.

Unarmed
Defeated
And lost.

Lydia Sargent (15)
South Wilts Grammar School for Girls, Salisbury

Remembering Last November

The way he smelt
The way he put his arm around me
His lasting smiles
Those deep green eyes
That's what did it

His shyness a blanket
Where we would wrap the silence around ourselves
Soft brown hair
A voice that cared
That's what did it

It was winter
You were cold
I fell into your warmth
Trapped in those eyes
I could not disguise
My hopes in a mirror
A mirror you hid
The warm fuzz of young love
Condensing on the glass

But I'll always remember
The way he smelt at the cinema.

Mei Ling Henry (14)
South Wilts Grammar School for Girls, Salisbury

Immortal

(Dedicated to my auntie)

From her eye she sheds a tear
The dampness that reveals her fear
She lies like rock, still and alone
Now emptiness is her only home.

Trapped in a world of desperation
Watching strangers' devastation
Grey haze fills her eyes, her sparkle is gone
Will this nightmare end anon?

She searches for memories amongst the dark
An endless journey to find a spark
She becomes the shell of what used to be
Once colourful and vibrant and full of glee.

Hanging on by a single thread
When it breaks she will feel no dread
For what she lives is a mortal hell
She waits forever for her life to expel.

The day arrives to set her free
Again colourful, vibrant and full of glee
Lost memories return, she emits a glow
She leaps to the sky where her happiness shall grow.

Clare Hillier (17)
South Wilts Grammar School for Girls, Salisbury

Miracles

The sun rises in the east and sets in the west
And Monday to Friday she walks past me
She doesn't notice me, huddled in my make-shift nest
I lie here trapped and she walks by, free

One day I'll talk to her, one day she'll notice me
Yet every morning she walks past and nothing happens
I feel that my life is one big decree
Where everything in my life is ruled to dampen

Then, one day she smiled at me and put some money
In my withered hat
I thought I would cry from the kindness
She continued to walk on past and that was that
But that was all I needed to prevent my heart
From turning loveless

For I am a homeless person
I see the world's beauty in different eyes
I smile and cry at the smallest of things
And thank God that compassion is still present

That miracles do happen.

Nadine Rowe (16)
South Wilts Grammar School for Girls, Salisbury

Melissa's Poem

Superhero Joe
With green bulbous eyes
He was quite handsome actually
Before he met the sky.

It was early one morning, that he woke and blew his nose
Then all of a sudden, fire came out and charred his bulbous toes
That was when he discovered he had some strange abilities.

He could breathe fire, grow hundreds of times his size
And even eat broccoli.
After cleaning up his ruined home, that had been crushed
With his growing size, he thought to himself
Because I can breathe fire, grow a hundred times my size
And even eat broccoli, maybe I could even fly like a superhero
And save lots kitties!'

Quite handsome, bulbous Joe, thought about the kitties in the trees
Stuck there crying all night and disturbing his wonderful dreams.

Silly Superhero Joe
He huffed and puffed and leapt as high as he could
But just fell back down
That's when he decided to jump off the highest building in town.

Wind was blowing everywhere and rain started to pour
It was like the scene in 'Titanic', he thought
But then he started to soar
It was quite unexpected and his quite handsome, bulbous eyes grew
As he neared the bottom of the building and that was when he knew
His eyes popped out of his quite handsome face and he sighed,
'It was very silly of me to try and fly so high.'

He woke up a day later, dressed in a costume
But it was just the cloth covering his whole body
That made him look like a mummy.

He woke a week later when his wrappings were taken off
Joe's poor, quite handsome face, was ruined
And he had prosthetic eyes.

Melissa Blair Denton (17)
South Wilts Grammar School for Girls, Salisbury

The Celebrity

Flashing lights. Cemented smiles.
Buckets of sequins and glitter.
Posing. Sideways. Front ways on.
The perfect celebrity picture.
Draped in jewels from head to toe.
Synthetic, shiny hair.
Shaking hands. Smile for the camera.
Stop for a moment. If you dare.
Designer outfits. Quality price tags.
Perfect shoes. Just a little too bright.
Ceaseless gossiping. Stories in the newspaper.
Constantly thrust into the spotlight.
Where will it end? The perfect celebrity.
Perhaps tomorrow, the next day or the next.
People think they know you.
Their judgements based on worthless text.
Nobody knows you. Not the real you.
You're only human. Just like the rest.
You just want a normal life. Perhaps a small family cottage.
You don't want to be the best.
But instead, they make you stand out.
Smother you in compliments.
Struggling. Struggling. To win an endless fight.
You feel exposed. Your faults highlighted.
You've gained too many pounds.
You've slept with too many. You got too drunk last night.
Who can you trust? Who can you hate?
Who believes that trash magazine?
Who is out to get you? To be cruel to be kind.
The press' latest scheme . . .
And yet caught up in the thicket of it all.
You long for the cameras. The bright lights.
Your agent's next call.

Sîan Kerley (14)
South Wilts Grammar School for Girls, Salisbury

Guilt Ease

One.
One solitary death.
One solitary life
One solitary figure, black clad,
Grieving alone.
The cold, spiteful rain leaving tracks down her cheeks
Stealing the role of her tears
Her salvation - that cruel salvation, stealing her affection,
As it stole her that night,
Drip, drip, drip the rain.
The cold, spiteful rain diluting her salvation
Her white fingers grip the glass again
As they had on that worst of days.
Her back is turned to their prying gaze.
Her fingers grip the glass
Her eyes closed. The grey orbs concealed
Concealing all correct emotion
The golden liquid. Her salvation
She dips her finger.
Drowning just one part of her denied sorrows
Lifting the drowned to her lips, she sadly smiles,
Finally, the first relief.
Silence. The rain is easing.
Her grief. Her guilt. Please . . . let it be easing
Drip, drip, drip, into her salvation.
Yet still tracks stain her cheeks. Not rain.
Anguished guilt. Her necessary guilt.
She clasps the glass to her. Remembering
Her fault. Her guilt. Her child
One mother,
One lonely life.
Grieving an undying death
Grieving into her salvation.

Freya Webb (14)
South Wilts Grammar School for Girls, Salisbury

Spring

Feel, the first when you take that breath
And then the walk, unsure but proud
The hesitant post babble speech
And the smiles of the parental figures

Learn, that excited step through the doors
The wide-eyed stare
As the world you know expands
To encompass these laughing, busy faces

Grow, the best friend, the male friend
That trip away from home
The life that makes you smile
The sun on your upturned face

Imagine, the world that could have been
The spirit you will be
The days ahead, though grudgingly counted
That first breath and the walk, unsure but proud.

Rachel Beagrie (15)
South Wilts Grammar School for Girls, Salisbury

Candy Cotton Sheets

Candy cotton sheets
Eulogies and epitaphs
Few words can kill me, they inspire in your hands
In freaks below, a savage plot of golden dust
And chariots of liars, a course waiting
For existence
I've made peace with God and burned the sage
And drank from the poison lake
Sewn your premonitions
Immaculate
Perfect killer
Playing perfumed God with clairvoyance.

Evie Kitt (15)
South Wilts Grammar School for Girls, Salisbury

Moving On . . .

Moving on . . . I began to wonder,
If you could find a better man?

I didn't believe what you said,
Walked away, left you for dead.

Laid awake all the night,
Longing for you to be alright.

The hardest things are what are right to say,
Let me turn back the time, to that day.

But it's too late to say sorry for all the things I have done
And all the victories I hadn't won.

Looking for the right words to find,
For all the questions on your mind.

The look on your face,
Filled me with shame and disgrace.

Please forgive me when I say,
I'm sorry for all that happened on that day.

Ruth-Megan Spreadbury (17)
South Wilts Grammar School for Girls, Salisbury

Adrenaline Rush

The spray hits my face
And I whoop, scream, with delight.
Here is where I'm home.

They don't understand,
No one can feel what I feel;
Me, the water, sunlight.

Adrenaline rush,
Pure, simple, not like I am.
Rhythm, rhyme, just right.

Splash! I'm over, in,
Laughing, the cold hits my skin.
An eternal fight

Between balance and flight,
It's never perfect.
You can't always win.

We're there, back upright
And away, gliding, sailing.
I pull the main in tight.

Catherine Honor (15)
South Wilts Grammar School for Girls, Salisbury

Poetry For The Logical

There should be a formula,
For writing poetry,
How else to know,
What goes where, or where to start?

X number of verses
Z number of lines
Rhyming couplets add up to 180°
Syllables are a sequence relating to n.

Pick a subject, then,
Look inside (this is the hard bit),
How do you feel?
Take it and square it.

Now plug it all in,
Press equals,
A poem, not a calculation.

Natasha Cowley (15)
South Wilts Grammar School for Girls, Salisbury

First Flight

Flying over the dark sea was just so different then,
Sitting on the small ledge,
Up high on the cliff top.

Once a small and fluffy chick,
He was now a graceful bird,
Skimming the ocean.

His descent to the ground
Was not quite as graceful as his flying now,
It had been more of a suicide flap,
But as he plunged to the ground,
He stretched out his wings
And flew.

Sophie Romain (11)
The Castle School, Thornbury

Chasing Freedom

The sun embeds itself in the murky
Bruised plum sky,
The jagged cliffs shelter Malawi
And her family,
Her crisp, subtle eyes gaze out
At the vast blue hue of the overwhelming ocean,
She has just escaped the slave trade
And was safe for the moment,
But she knew her freedom
Was balancing on a knife's edge,
A sharp, cruel knife with no mercy,
A glistening tear sheds down
And lands on her maroon gnarled skirt,
Sparing the thought about the others,
The violence,
The abuse,
The neglect,
The desperation,
She knew it sounded childish, but it was true,
It wasn't fair,
She felt greedy,
All the slaves being abused
And she was sitting out here
Gazing at the beautiful crisp, Indian Ocean,
She was free,
For now.

Kiddie Sheikh (12) & Sam Steele (11)
The Castle School, Thornbury

If Humans Could Talk (In A Cat's World!)

If humans could talk
What would they say?
Well, they're not horses,
So they wouldn't say *neigh*.

They're definitely not dogs
'Cause they don't chase us
And when they're around,
We don't run in a bus!

When we miaow,
For some food,
They get a bit confused . . .

When I want to get in,
They open the door
And then I don't want
To be in anymore!

They're obviously not us,
Because they last a lot longer,
But we've got nine lives,
So we're so much stronger.

So now I know
What humans can talk,
But I've got to go now,
I've got to take my human for a walk!

Paige Sanders (12) & Cate Welmers (12)
The Castle School, Thornbury

Wanting A Home

I was in my cage all alone
I only had my freezing cold bone
Then all the dogs started to whine
Because they wanted it to be feeding time
All the humans came
They all did the same
Umming and *ahhing*
Ooing and *booing*
What about this dog?
What about that dog?
After all the fuss
It was walkie time for all of us
We went up and down
Round and round
Forwards and backwards
This way, that way
When we were back to boring home
I went to find my bone
It was in my warm, cosy bed
Then I stood up and said,
'Don't be sad, we will all get homes
And sit in front of the fire and chew our bones'
Then someone came for me
Two human bears looked down at me
The bears bent down and cuddled me
And they decided that I was their one to be.

Katie Walker (12)
The Castle School, Thornbury

What I Hope The Future Will Be

The sun's crispy golden face,
Peered down on the pale hue of jade grass.

Aid is coming for those who need it,
This feels like a crime we didn't commit.

Hours pass, the formidable force of the sun
Takes its toll on the suffering people,
Crisp, flaky mud surrounds the barren landscape,
Sadly, there's no way to escape.

Aid is coming for those who need it,
This feels like a crime we didn't commit.

The water's subtle complexity
Boils into the humid atmosphere
Wasted. Gone.

Aid is coming for those who need it,
This feels like a crime we didn't commit.

Trucks emerge on the plum-purple horizon,
'Hurry, come on, don't take too long.'
People mutter along with a splutter.

Aid is coming for those who need it,
This feels like a crime we didn't commit.

Aid finally arrives along with a surprise:
Medicine, water, food and two goats,
These are the building blocks of life!

Sam Crow (12) & Ryan Waite (11)
The Castle School, Thornbury

A Dolphin's Great Life

My grey skin, so smooth and tough,
Twisting and turning in the glowing sea.
Gliding through the sea so rough,
Shells crackle as the fish swim with glee.

The sun blows like diamonds down on us,
I can see some dinner waiting for me.
I'm going to snatch it quick without any fuss,
Being a happy animal in the big blue sea.

My teeth are sharp and white,
With my eyes big and bright.
Even though I never bite,
My skin shimmers in the light.

We try and get away from the bad,
But they can catch you up quick.
They take our friends and make us sad,
Apparently they make them sick.

I love my home, it is so great,
I'm as happy as I could be.
I go here and there and never be late,
But a dolphin certainly suits me.

Hannah Moore (12)
The Castle School, Thornbury

Saved Tigers

I walk through a whirling vortex, then
I'm in the year 1900 in India
I ask a villager where the king lives.

As I walk up
The steps to the doors
Of the king's house
I knock on the door and go in.

I ask why he
Kills tigers and he
Said they are
Bloodthirsty creatures.

They're not, they're not, I said
They won't hurt you
If you don't hurt them.

The king agreed
And I went back
To the present day
And there are still loads of tigers left.

Sam Mindenhall (11)
The Castle School, Thornbury

If I Could Go Back In Time!

It would be wonderful if I could go back in time
And see the first dinosaur; a new world sublime.

All the dodos, mammoths and beasts that have died,
Could be brought to the present, so they would have survived.
No more piecing together a strange bone set,
Or guessing how this animal lived and ate.

Listening to those scientists with our knowledge today,
Maybe we could help them to take disease away.

We could listen to Shakespeare and watch his magical plays,
About monsters and witches in historical days.
Or watch Da Vinci paint the Mona Lisa's smile
And discover the mystery in a short while.

The world wars could be stopped and guns taken away,
This would make the world better; we could all shout, 'Hooray!'

We would know about pollution and could stop that as well
And in years to come, our sons and daughters would tell
Of how one boy changed the world for the good of mankind,
Pain and death would be put behind.

Richard Timbrell (11)
The Castle School, Thornbury

The Sea's Voice

I am the voice of the sea
That lives with great pride
Riding on thy royal sea horses
On thy tide of a thousand dreams

Day and night I am restless
Spraying waves everywhere
And when out surfing or bodyboarding
You may see me riding, riding, riding
Across the ocean blue water

If there were one I would change
With all thy greatest desire
Is to cast thy tsunami
Back to great slumber

But that nightmare is now past
It is now history's grasp
So if thee happen to be on the beach
Look out to see me riding, riding, riding
For I am the restless sea.

Paul James Long (12)
The Castle School, Thornbury

My Pony's Diary

I'm stuck in my stable,
There's nothing much to do,
I've got laminitis
And I'm sedated too.

There's powder in my feed
And water in my hay,
I'm on Bute, Sedalin
And Bromide twice a day.

I'm kicking at my door
And pawing at the ground,
Mucking up my bedding
And pacing round and round.

Now I'm growing frantic,
This really isn't me,
I'm getting really wild,
I'm desperate to be free.

Hannah Cornford (12)
The Castle School, Thornbury

Baby William

I have this baby cousin,
His name is Baby Will,
He was born on the 14th of May,
Which was a very good day,
He has a big brother, Ollie,
Who is very jolly,
His mum and dad,
Were very glad
And that is Baby Will!

Helen Walpole (11)
Westonbirt School, Tetbury

If

If my dog were a drink
She would be champagne
All bubbly with excitement

If my dog were another animal
She would be a kangaroo
All jumpy and lively

If my dog were a teddy bear
She would be *big*
Cute and cuddly

If my dog were a flower
She would be a daisy
Small but sweet

If my dog were a colour
She would be yellow
Brightening up my day!

Cassie Jane Greenhill (12)
Westonbirt School, Tetbury

If

If my sister wasn't her,
She would be a kangaroo,
She is bouncy and wild
And needs to be returned to the zoo!

If my sister wasn't her
She would be a bowl of noodles,
There is loads of her everywhere
And her hair's as mad as poodles!

If my sister wasn't her,
She'd be a sea cruiser,
Here, there, everywhere,
As out of control as a bulldozer!

Lucy Fenn (12)
Westonbirt School, Tetbury

Come With Me

Come with me,
Take my hand,
Close your eyes,
Let's leave this land.

Come with me,
Far away,
Leave your home,
Leave your play.

Come with me,
Around the bend,
I promise you,
That I'm your friend.

You came with me,
You took my hand,
You closed your eyes,
We've left that land.

Lydia Marshall (11)
Westonbirt School, Tetbury

What Do I Do?

I'm cheerful,
What do I do?
I'm dispirited,
What do I do?
I'm embarrassed,
What do I do?
I'm scared,
What do I do?
I'm nervous,
What do I do?
I've found you,
I know what to do!

Megan Mardon (13)
Westonbirt School, Tetbury

Black And White

The black thing's in the corner,
The white thing's in the room,
The buzzing all around me,
When people are arriving soon,
I lie in the corner,
The black, dark corner and wait!

The black paint in the corner,
The white paint in the room,
The coolness of the darkness
And soothing music blues,
I lie in the frosty window,
The black sky coming through,
I sit peacefully waiting in the gloom.

The white thing's in the corner,
The black thing's in the room,
The party in the back room,
My white clothes shining blue,
I feel more colour coming,
But darkness when I move.

Emma Gardner (12)
Westonbirt School, Tetbury

Pink And Orange

These colours may clash,
If they do, they turn into a horrible rash,
I put this into horrible thought
And if I didn't, I may have been taught.

These are not the only colours that clash,
Or the ones that turn into a rash,
If you put them to the test,
They turn into a horrible pest.

If you see them
You may have to dash
And that's the end
Of my horrible rash.

Hester Ingram (11)
Westonbirt School, Tetbury

Young Writers Information

We hope you have enjoyed reading this book - and that you will continue to enjoy it in the coming years.

If you like reading and writing poetry drop us a line, or give us a call, and we'll send you a free information pack.

Alternatively if you would like to order further copies of this book or any of our other titles, then please give us a call or log onto our website at
www.youngwriters.co.uk

Young Writers Information
Remus House
Coltsfoot Drive
Peterborough
PE2 9JX

(01733) 890066